D0103759

After the Boxes Are Unpacked

Moving On After Moving In

⇜ SUSAN MILLER ⇝

TYNDALE HOUSE PUBLISHERS, INC.
CAROL STREAM, ILLINOIS

After the Boxes Are Unpacked: Moving On After Moving In
© 1995, 2016 by Susan Miller

A Focus on the Family book published by Tyndale House Publishers, Inc., Carol Stream, Illinois 60188

Focus on the Family and the accompanying logo and design are federally registered trademarks of Focus on the Family, 8605 Explorer Drive, Colorado Springs, CO 80920.

TYNDALE and Tyndale's quill logo are registered trademarks of Tyndale House Publishers, Inc.

No part of this publication may be reproduced, stored in a retrieval system, or transmitted in any form or by any means—electronic, mechanical, photocopy, recording, or otherwise—without prior written permission of Focus on the Family.

Unless otherwise indicated, all Scripture quotations are taken from the *New American Standard Bible.*® Copyright © 1960, 1962, 1963, 1968, 1971, 1972, 1973, 1975, 1977, 1995 by The Lockman Foundation. Used by permission. (www.Lockman.org).

Scripture quotations marked KJV are taken from the *Holy Bible*, King James Version.

Scripture quotations marked NLT are taken from the *Holy Bible*, New Living Translation, copyright © 1996, 2004, 2015 by Tyndale House Foundation. Used by permission of Tyndale House Publishers, Inc., Carol Stream, Illinois 60188. All rights reserved.

Scripture quotations marked NLV are taken from the Holy Bible, New Life Version. Copyright © 1969–2003 by Christian Literature International, P. O. Box 777, Canby, OR 97013. Used by permission.

Scripture quotations marked TLB are taken from *The Living Bible* [paraphrase], copyright © 1971 by Tyndale House Foundation. Used by permission of Tyndale House Publishers, Inc., Carol Stream, Illinois 60188. All rights reserved.

Some stories presented in this book are composites based on the author's experience and interaction with hundreds of women who have been uprooted by a move. Any resemblance to actual persons is coincidental.

Some people's names and certain details of their stories have been changed to protect the privacy of the individuals involved. However, the facts of what happened and the underlying principles have been conveyed as accurately as possible.

The use of material from or references to various websites does not imply endorsement of those sites in their entirety. Availability of websites and pages is subject to change without notice.

Editor: Liz Duckworth

Cover design by Beth Sparkman

Cover illustration by Ruth Pizzi. Copyright © Tyndale House Publishers, Inc. All rights reserved.

For information about special discounts for bulk purchases, please contact Tyndale House Publishers at csresponse@tyndale.com, or call 1-800-323-9400.

Library of Congress Cataloging-in-Publication Data
Names: Miller, Susan, date- author
Title: After the boxes are unpacked : moving on after moving in / Susan Miller.
Description: First Edition | Carol Stream, Illinois : Tyndale House Publishers, 2016. |
   Originally published: Colorado Springs, Colo. : Focus on the Family Pub., 1995. | "A Focus
   on the Family book." | Includes bibliographical references and index.
Identifiers: LCCN 2016016028 | ISBN 9781589978720 (alk. paper)
Subjects: LCSH: Women—Religious life. | Moving, Household—Religious
   aspects—Christianity.
Classification: LCC BV4527.M54 2016 | DDC 248.8/43—dc23 LC record available at
   https://lccn.loc.gov/2016016028

Printed in the United States of America

25   24   23   22   21   20   19
9   8   7   6   5   4   3

In memory of Bill

Twenty years ago I dedicated the first edition of this book to my beloved husband with the words, "I'd follow you to the ends of the earth." One day, I'll follow you to our eternal home, and we will be together again.

Praise for *After the Boxes Are Unpacked*

There's a reason why moving to a new area is ranked on stress tests at the same level as the death of a spouse. It's an emotional hot zone—even if you're moving to a place and opportunity you're excited about. It often takes years for a new address to provide the kind of sanctuary our hearts long for. In the meantime, the pressure on everyone in the family picture can feel enormous. Fortunately, someone has stepped forward with a plan that takes the sting out of moving and accelerates the time it takes to turn a new location into an emotional and relational haven. You're going to feel much more at home after you've read Susan Miller's book *After the Boxes Are Unpacked*.

> DR. TIM KIMMEL
> Author, *Grace Based Parenting* and *Grace Filled Marriage*

We moved eighteen times in twenty-three years, and to say it was a challenge is a gross understatement. After I discovered Susan Miller's book *After the Boxes Are Unpacked*, it made the rest of those moves smoother. In this new edition of her book, Susan not only shares new strategies available to those who move, but she also addresses the psychological aspect of making those moves. This is the most comprehensive and definitive book about moving and making that move more effectively.

Susan helps the reader journey from the sadness and loss of a move into a mind-set of enthusiasm and hope. If you want to be the most content you can be when it comes to your next move, then read this book.

> ELLIE KAY
> America's Family Financial Expert ® and bestselling author of *Heroes at Home*

Sometimes moving can leave you feeling as empty as the corrugated boxes you've tossed away, but Susan Miller's book *After the Boxes Are Unpacked* gives you hope! From finding a new doctor to making new friends, Susan Miller shares encouraging, heartwarming stories of women who've "been there and felt that" when moving. She provides practical action steps that help you move forward in your new surroundings. This is a must-read for every woman who finds herself relocating to a new community.

SHARON JAYNES
Author, *The Power of a Woman's Words*

As our song proclaims, "The Army goes rolling along," and so do the spouse, the kids, the pets, and all the emotions with the news of another PCS. As a chaplain, I have had the privilege of using Susan's book *After the Boxes Are Unpacked* for families across the globe. Susan has been our conference speaker in Korea, Hawaii, and Germany. Everyone should experience a move and read *After the Boxes Are Unpacked*, and see what God will do in his or her life. Don't PCS without it!

US ARMY CHAPLAIN LT. COL. KENT WALKER AND
SHAWNA WALKER

Contents

Foreword

FOR MANY COUPLES, their major goal in moving is to stay married! For singles, the need is to maintain their sanity—and to find that "special friend" with a truck! Moving isn't easy. As someone who has packed too many haul-it-yourself trucks in his time, I know that moving can rank right up there with wallpapering, root canals, pet-sitting a pit bull, and having your six-month-old triplets all start to teethe at the same time. *But* it isn't just the physical exhaustion that's the real challenge in moving. It's *emotionally unpacking* that can hurt long after the sore muscles have healed.

The *real help* you need after the boxes show up at your new place is what this book is so incredible at providing. Here, in this revised and updated edition of what's become a family classic, you'll learn how to close loops and start anew. How to help your children do more than just mope around, how *you* can find and be a new friend, and how *you* can move forward as a person, spouse, and family. Reading Susan's book is like having a world-class coach show up at your door the day you found out you were really moving. She brings her wisdom and encouragement to take the pain out of having to pack, the smarting out of having to uproot the kids, and the sting out of leaving family and friends. And once you get to your new destination, like a personalized welcome service, Susan Miller will provide biblical advice and clearheaded counsel to guide you through the many adjustments still to come, months after everything is on the shelf.

Believe me, Susan's been there. She and Bill, her husband, moved more than a dozen times. She knows the financial, emotional, and spiritual challenges that come with a change of address. She knows what it's like to leave parents and best friends, search for a new church, hunt down a seemingly nonexistent reasonable rental home, and find a doctor in a strange city at midnight. More than that, she knows how to grow spiritually during those times of incredible transition, as well as where to find the courage to put down roots all over again. Even if you just had to move a few months ago! Or the place you're going isn't like *anywhere* you've ever been! In your hand is hope and help.

Not only has Susan lived out the principles you'll learn in this powerful, hands-on resource, but she has also taught them to hundreds of people just like you. Susan's ministry has been a wonderful success. Her program has been used by churches across the country, and I think it should be a required ministry in every church that's serious about welcoming newcomers.

Over the years, I've had the privilege of helping a number of authors develop their books. The authors I've worked with all have three traits. First, I only work with people I know personally and believe in whole-heartedly. Second, they have to be people who have long-term track records of serving and loving the Lord and who can clearly articulate that love to others. And third, they have to be able to put practical, biblical help within easy reach of those experiencing a heartfelt need.

Susan Miller fits all those criteria. It's an honor for me to recommend her to you as a wonderfully talented author with words of hope for those soon to face, or already dealing with, all the trauma and uncertainty that goes with transition. This book, like all of Susan's books, will build your faith and strengthen your family *and* help you get the boxes unpacked!

God's best to you,

JOHN TRENT, PhD
Gary D. Chapman Chair of Marriage and Family Ministry and Therapy
    at Moody Theological Seminary

Acknowledgments

FROM THE CLASSIC MOVIE *Enchanted April*, I vividly recall the line, "No one should ever write a book that God wouldn't like to read." My goal in writing this book was to make sure God *would* want to read it and that it would bring glory and honor to His name.

I could not have made it to the finish line without the many people who accompanied me on the journey of writing this book twenty years ago and those who continued the journey with me as I revised and updated it.

John Trent, from the beginning of my ministry to newcomers at Scottsdale Bible Church, you encouraged me to write this book, opened the door for me to do it, and then held my hand through the process. Thank you for all you did to make my dream a reality.

Larry Weeden, you were the first person at Focus on the Family who encouraged my writing. I was so excited to visit with you for my first "book talk," I slid down the banister in the lobby with glee. Little did I know you would become my friend for over twenty years. And now, once again, you have encouraged me with writing this revised, updated edition. Thank you for believing in me and in the timeless message of this book.

Liz Duckworth, my gifted Focus on the Family editor. I could not have asked for anyone more thorough and articulate to edit this book. Thank you for embracing this project with sensitivity, never losing my voice in your editing. You have been a blessing both professionally and personally.

Carol Eidson and *Dante Miro* from Focus on the Family and *Amie Carlson, Kim Miller, Annette Hayward,* and *Sue Thompson* from Tyndale House Publishing—my deepest appreciation to each of you, and the many other team members, for your invaluable part in making this book happen.

Al Janssen and Gwen Ellis, during your time at Focus on the Family, you were an intricate part of making this book possible. I am so grateful that you caught the vision.

Jerry and Nancy West, faithful friends across the miles and over the years. When we moved from Atlanta, your friendship was the story that began this book. You taught me that friendship can deepen and grow, regardless of time and distance. You will always hold a special place in my heart.

Nancy Del Duca, when I first started writing, you believed in me when I didn't believe in myself. You encouraged me day and night through each chapter. You continue to instill in me the words, "I can do this." I treasure you.

Sudie Althisar and Sandy Richmond, you teamed with me to start the first Newcomers' Ministry at Scottsdale Bible Church. You helped me fine-tune the teaching material and became a part of the inception of this book.

Jackie Oesch, you gave me the first opportunity to expand my ministry in other churches across the nation. As I updated this book, your prayers and steadfast friendship encouraged me beyond measure.

Wayne and Bev Lehsten, Bob and Mary Malouf, your biblical wisdom kept me centered within the pages of this book and keeps me centered in the pages of my life.

Karen Erickson, long ago you were a voice in my ear that said, "You need to write a book."

My incredible staff at Just Moved Ministry—Ann Kelley, Joan Langston, Trina Lowery, Donna Ludwig, Jill Maher, Dina Matthews, Paulette Miller, JoAnn Smith (and our two movers: Sharon Nowlin and

Keri Johnson)—it's a privilege and honor to serve with such an amazing team of dedicated, committed, devoted, and selfless women who so passionately love God and our ministry. I stand on your shoulders of excellence. You make me look a whole lot better than I am and enable me to do a whole lot more than I could have imagined. Sharing ministry and life with you is one of my greatest joys.

Ann Kelley, the greatest gift a writer can have. You are a skilled editor and wordsmith who combed every word and every endless detail, made my fragmented and disjointed sentences whole, offered fabulous suggestions, updated words and phrases, and walked with me to the finish line of revising and updating this book. God smiled on me the day you came into my life.

Joan Langston, you've been by my side, overseeing Just Moved Ministry from the very beginning. Just Moved couldn't have functioned, and wouldn't be where it is today, without you—and neither would I. You are God's incredible gift and blessing to me and to our ministry.

Paulette Miller, you are invaluable to me in countless ways. The day you volunteered to be my personal assistant was life-changing for me in ministry. Thank you for being available 24-7 with a devoted servant's heart. I cherish you.

Jane O'Connell and Mary Furniss, your faithfulness and loyalty in serving our ministry have been key in implementing our mission and vision. You have kept us on track and focused. I am grateful to you and for you.

Our ministry prayer team and my endless circle of prayer warriors, your prayers are the strong foundation for our kingdom outreach. Thank you for faithfully circling our ministry in prayer and for standing in the gap for me.

The countless volunteers in our office and all over the world, you are the hands and feet of our ministry and this book. Without you, we wouldn't be able to touch so many lives for Christ. I value each and every one of you.

All my "moving friends" who shared their stories, their insights, their joys, and their struggles with moving. You have given life to the pages.

My son, Bill, and daughter, Ginger, you are the joy of my life. You have made your daddy proud. Thank you for carrying on his tradition of being my number one cheerleaders. You have been the wind beneath my broken wings.

Ann and James, you are my favorite daughter-in-law and son-in-law! I think of you as another daughter and son. Thank you for loving Bill and Ginger.

Mackenzie and Morgan, Austin, Savannah, Steven, and C. J., my amazing grandchildren! My prayer is that this book will reveal Christ to you in a way that will draw you closer to Him.

And to Bill, my beloved husband and soul mate for forty-five years. You are written all over my life and the pages of this book.

Introduction

HAVE YOU RECENTLY moved or prepared to move, or do you still feel unsettled since you moved? I promise you are not alone. There are millions of women like you, experiencing the life-changing effects of being uprooted by a move.

According to a US Census Bureau report, the number of women in the United States who moved in one year was 18.3 million! There were nearly 36 million men, women, and children in the United States who moved during that time frame.[1]

For many women, being uprooted and going through a tangible loss can be overwhelming. If you are single, divorced, or widowed, the experience is even more difficult without a support system.

Some of the biggest challenges you face when you move involve leaving behind family, friends, a home, and familiar surroundings that were a part of your life. You might feel disconnected, disillusioned, or discouraged. Perhaps you even feel a great sense of spiritual confusion and doubt. Women go through a range of emotions as they experience the stages of loss and grief.

I refer to moving as a "closet illness" because so many women have said to me, "I didn't know anyone else felt like this." "I thought something was wrong with me because I dreaded the thought of moving." "I resented being relocated and uprooted." "I thought I was the only one going through this kind of stress." Research has shown that moving is one of the top five reasons for stress. No wonder you feel the way you do!

In the pages that follow, there is hope and encouragement to get you through the major impact of a move. I've worked with hundreds of women just like you and equipped them with the tools for a smoother transition. In each chapter I'll be giving you biblical principles and practical application to guide you through your move, and I'll walk with you through the process. I'll share what I've learned through my own experiences in moving, along with the wisdom I've gained from over twenty years of teaching and counseling women who have faced the same circumstances. Throughout the book, I'll draw from a reservoir of my "moving friends" who have so graciously shared their stories, tips, and ideas to help women like you through the transition of moving.

You'll get through this; I'll show you how.

Cheering You On—Some Things You Need to Know

I am delighted that Focus on the Family has given me the opportunity to update *After the Boxes Are Unpacked* after twenty years in print and over 100,000 copies sold!

The upheaval of moving, the application of biblical principles, and the three-step process to let go, start over, and move forward are timeless and will not change in this updated edition.

It is my desire to capture a whole new generation of movers facing daily change in a mobile society. There are issues and challenges a mover faces today that she didn't have twenty years ago. I want to seize this opportunity to wrap the unchanging Word of God around the lives of movers in a changing world and to ensure a stable home foundation in the midst of being uprooted.

For the last twenty years, I have been in full-time ministry to women and families uprooted and displaced by relocation. This has given me far greater experience, knowledge, and insight into the emotional and spiritual needs of movers today. Traveling all over the world to bring women the encouragement and hope of Jesus Christ keeps me on the cutting edge of their struggles, stories, issues, and daily challenges.

New, in this edition, is a greater development of the unique challenges faced by corporate expats, the "trailing spouse," the wives of professional athletes, missionaries, and the single, widowed, divorced, and retired mover. I'll introduce the "crisis move" and the way it affects the family, as well as share stories of inspiration from military spouses who are all too familiar with frequent moves. I will offer ways to reach out to women and families who have moved into your community—even to those who may not share your beliefs, cultural lifestyle, or value system.

In the back of the book, you'll find Focus on the Family's "Twelve Traits of a Healthy Family." These traits are reflected throughout this book as they relate to the impact of a move on a family.

On a personal note . . . when I wrote this book more than twenty years ago, my husband, Bill, was as much a part of each page as I was. His daily encouragement was a stepping stone from one chapter to another, and our stories gave insight into our marriage and our unconditional love for each other in the midst of our moves.

When Bill lost a painful four-month battle with cancer, my life became uprooted in ways I'd never experienced before. The loss took me to a deeper understanding of what it takes to survive a major life crisis and life change. The biblical principles I'd discovered to survive my many moves and shared in this book held true as I lived with this painful loss. Though this book is about moving, it is relevant to all the changes in life and the loss we experience. How I began to let go, start over, and move forward after Bill's death is reflected throughout the chapters and can be applied to any major life change you might be going through.

In updating this book I could not leave out our stories and my many references to Bill. Little did Bill know that he would still be a part of each page, but this time I will feel him looking over my shoulder as I encourage you all the more with how to survive change and loss in life.

PART 1

Let Go

My home address? Christ.
In Him I dwell, wherever else I be.
As bird in the air, as branch in the vine,
as tree in the soil, as fish in the sea.
He is my home.
My business address?
Here.
Little piney cove or London, Corinth,
Calcutta or Rome, Shanghai or Paris.
My business address?
Wherever He puts me,
but He is my home.[1]

RUTH BELL GRAHAM

CHAPTER I

FROM GRITS TO GUACAMOLE

For though I am far away from you my heart is with you.
COLOSSIANS 2:5, TLB

THEN . . . It was four o'clock in the morning and just beginning to sprinkle rain as we walked down the driveway to our van. Bill and I, and our two children, were facing another journey into the unknown. In order to leave our house empty and clean for the new owners, dear friends let us spend the night with them. We fought back tears as we realized our lives would never again be so daily connected. As we exchanged hugs and said our good-byes at the end of the driveway, the pain of loss and separation became real. The rain began pouring down as we rushed into the van, not lingering to form the words that stuck in our throats. Silently we asked ourselves the question, *When will we see each other again?*

Once in the van, I rolled down the window to my friend Nancy. Our faces almost touching, our eyes brimming with tears, I whispered, "I just don't know if I can do this one more time!"

Nancy answered encouragingly, "Yes, you can, and you will—with

God's help. Now go!" I quickly rolled up the window, and as we pulled away, I held back tears of sorrow. I reassured Bill and the children that I was going to be okay. I knew in my heart that somehow I had to find it in myself, once again, to let go of all that was near and dear, and to start over, moving ahead with a new life.

As we began our long journey westward, I reflected on all of our previous moves. Some had been good—a chance for a new beginning, a fresh start. Some had been a part of Bill's climb up the ladder of success. Some had been easy and others hard—especially as our children got older.

Moving is more than loading and unloading boxes. It is leaving behind everything familiar to face the unfamiliar.

When we moved, countless questions filled my thoughts: How am I going to find new doctors? Where are the best grocery stores? When is garbage pickup day? Who will I call if I need a plumber or an electrician? Which radio station will have the best country music? How will I begin to find trusted babysitters?

Finding answers to a list of simple questions was always a concern and worry to me. The big questions were overwhelming to even think about: Did we make the right decision about where to live? Where do we find a new church home? Will we have good neighbors? Will the schools be good? What about making new friends? *Oh, the effort and energy it will take!*

I looked in my rear view mirror and began to focus on everything I left behind. How could I start over when I hadn't even begun to let go of everyone and everything I loved? I felt the loneliness of being so far away from family and friends creep in. I felt the guilt of leaving behind Mama, who had been very ill. I felt anger and resentment as I asked, *Why do we have to move again? Why do we have to move so far away from all that I am and all that I identify with?* I fought back the familiar depression and the dread of the unknown that clouded my mind.

My thoughts switched back to the present. The bags really were packed and the van really was loaded down with valuables that couldn't be shipped ahead. The rest of life was in brown boxes in a moving van headed for a destination two thousand miles away. Once again I was pulling up stakes. Once again I was saying good-bye to friends. At this moment, I didn't belong anywhere—not in Atlanta, our old city, and certainly not in Phoenix, our new home, which seemed a million miles away. The emptiness overwhelmed me.

This was our thirteenth move in eighteen years of marriage. Bill was climbing the corporate ladder in hotel and restaurant management, and moving came with the profession. It also became a recurring part of our life together.

I smiled for the children's sake, to give them a sense of security that everything was going to be all right. I engaged in some meaningful conversation with Bill, to assure him I was indeed standing by his side in this corporate transfer and was united with him in this move.

Hours drifted by. I woke up from a nap that had been induced by the emotions of good-byes and leaving Atlanta. The sun was beginning to shine and the rain had stopped. The air was fresh and the day felt new in the early morning dawn. With the breaking of day came hope for tomorrow and renewed optimism to overcome new challenges. A smile came, not only to my face, but to my heart, and I felt a sense of God's peace. The Lord had been my Rock for thirteen moves, and together we could do this again.

He was the Friend who would go with me. He would ease my hurt and bring me contentment. God would never leave me. I knew He was already at my destination, waiting with open arms.

Little did I know at the time that this move would have a profound impact on my life and become the catalyst for this book.

A reassuring Scripture verse came to mind: "Don't be afraid, for the Lord will go before you and will be with you; he will not fail nor forsake you" (Deuteronomy 31:8, TLB). I leaned over, kissed Bill on the cheek, and broke the silence by saying, "This is a beautiful day to begin a new journey together." I took a deep breath, and in the quietness of my heart, said to myself, *Yes, Lord, I am going to make it one more time!*

Westward Ho!

On our journey to Phoenix, we looked like the notorious Griswold family from the National Lampoon film series with our loaded van, two children, one dog, six pieces of luggage strapped on the top, and a U-Haul trailer in tow carrying all my plants. (We always try to hold on to everything and take it all with us, don't we?) Of course, I didn't realize that after three days in the U-Haul with the summer heat and no air, all my plants would be dead when we arrived.

We arrived in August, the hottest month of the year. I cried the entire month. I couldn't get used to seeing all those rocks in yards, some of which were even painted green to look like grass! *And where was everybody?* How was I to know they had all left Phoenix to get out of the 120-degree heat?

Bill and I had come to Phoenix previously, in July, for a weekend house-hunting trip. Those three-day decision-making trips never allow enough time to know the area where you want to live. There's never enough time to find the best schools and a house you can afford that will hold all your furniture. Needless to say, we didn't find anything on that trip; so when Bill went on ahead of us to start work, he bought a house I had never seen before arriving in Phoenix. We lived in a hotel for two weeks, waiting for the house to close. Of course, you know what that's like—the glamour wears off quickly!

All the things I had to do raced through my mind. I knew I needed to get everything squared away by myself because Bill would be preoccupied with his new job.

The first thing I did was to make our children's transition as smooth as possible. I knew it was crucial that they get settled in quickly, so I registered them not only in school, but on soccer teams, since they both had played in Atlanta. They started practice before we even moved into our house.

Bill *was* preoccupied with his new job and started traveling immediately. I spent the days trying to learn which streets would take me where I wanted to go and how to get back to the place from where I started. I used the time while we were still in the hotel to make all the necessary arrangements and appointments to get the house up and running.

With Bill and the children settled into a routine, it was time to tackle the house itself. The empty rooms chilled me, despite the 120-degree heat. The big moving van containing the bulk of our furnishings arrived, and the movers dumped furniture and boxes carelessly in each room. I was left to take each pile of stuff and, once again, make this house a home for us. Slowly, as I unpacked each box, hung the pictures, added a few new plants, and placed accessories and cherished mementos in each room, I began to feel comforted by all that was familiar.

By the time the house was settled, school had started. Bill was entrenched in his work, and I set out to find my niche in Scottsdale, the area near Phoenix where we had settled.

I soon learned Scottsdale was referred to as "La La Land," the home of the rich and the famous. I certainly didn't feel like a "La La Lady"! It seemed everyone played tennis and golf, or jogged in cute little outfits with cute little figures to match. I was already emotionally fragile from the move, overly sensitive to the spider veins in my legs, painfully conscious of my "thunder thighs," and totally aware of the extra pounds I was always trying to lose. My self-image was pretty low. I didn't seem to measure up.

I remembered how moving always created a loss of identity and affected my self-esteem.

Once again I thought, *If I don't get involved, it won't matter, and it will just be easier when we leave the next time.*

All our previous moves had been within the Southern states. Born in South Carolina, I had never been so far away from my deep Southern roots. What I knew of the West was only that I'd be eating guacamole instead of grits. I struggled with living in a world where my Southern heritage and Southern accent didn't fit. I was terribly homesick and missed the close relationships of family and friends.

Part of me anticipated the opportunities a new place would offer, and part of me was sad to leave behind our family, our church, established friendships, and our Southern roots. Still another part of me was just plain weary. I wanted to be like the tiny doodlebug that hides by burying itself in the sand. The thought of moving to a new place and starting all over again was both challenging and depressing.

Sometimes it's hard to see God in the midst of our circumstances. When we ventured west, I went through a whole lot of "Why, God?" and "Where are You in all of this?" And yet, I knew He had always been with us, whether or not we saw Him in the midst of our chaos, or even if we didn't have all the answers to "why."

I knew that coming to Scottsdale was part of God's plan for our family. Yet I also knew there were plenty of changes that needed to take place in me before I could even begin to call this place home. In my twenties, I had rededicated my life to Christ. In my thirties, we were baptized together as a family, and in my forties it was as if God said, *Go west and grow!* "For I know the plans I have for you, says the Lord. They are plans for good and not for evil, to give you a future and a hope" (Jeremiah 29:11, TLB).

When our family moves, finding a church is one of the first things we do to begin to put down roots. We visited many churches before we settled at Scottsdale Bible Church. There our life as a couple and as a family was enriched and we began to grow in our relationships with Jesus Christ. It was there Christ became the *center* of our lives, not just a sidebar to our lives.

As my security in Christ deepened, my self-image began to change. I only wanted to measure up to God's principles, not the principles of those around me. Gradually, my feelings of inadequacy were replaced with an adequacy found in Christ and through His Word.

By moving me to the desert, God was quenching a thirst in my heart that only He could fill.

Do not call to mind the former things,
Or ponder things of the past.
Behold, I will do something new,
Now it will spring forth;

Will you not be aware of it?
I will even make a roadway in the wilderness,
Rivers in the desert.
ISAIAH 43:18-19

And indeed He did.

Now . . . so much remains the same, and so much has changed since moving to Arizona.

I still live in Scottsdale but have moved twice since we bought our first home.

I still go to Scottsdale Bible Church, where I have taught the Moving On After Moving In class for twenty-five years to hundreds of women new to the area.

I still don't play tennis or golf, but I am great at kickboxing and Zumba.

My spider veins and thunder thighs have gotten a little worse with age, but on a hot day you'll find me in shorts. As far as losing a few pounds, well, they come and they go.

My circle of friends extends all over the world with Just Moved Ministry, but I still cherish my circle of dear friends from Atlanta.

My Southern roots will always be a part of who I am, but my Western roots are a part of who I have become.

I still love to plant flowers and have a yard full of geraniums.

I also love to plant seeds of encouragement and hope in Jesus Christ as I speak all over the world.

I still love grits, but guacamole is definitely a favorite.

I still miss oak trees, but there's nothing like a cactus in full bloom.

I might have rocks in my front yard, but I have compromised with green grass in my backyard.

I still stumble through speaking Spanish but know enough words to be gracious to another culture.

Our two children are grown and married. Bill Jr. and his family live in Atlanta, and Ginger and her family live in Gilbert, about thirty minutes from me.

I have six amazing grandchildren who fill my life with joy and memories.

I founded Just Moved Ministry in 1995, and it's become a global outreach to uprooted women, touching the lives of thousands of women and families for Christ.

After forty-five years of marriage, I still love Bill, even though he's gone home to be with the Lord.

And I still love Jesus. More now than I did then!

Steps to Survive a Move

Maybe you are where I have been: grieving over leaving family and friends, concerned about a broken relationship or the stress on your marriage, worried about your children's adjustment, confused about knowing which doctor to call, wondering where to find the right church, or simply overwhelmed by all the tasks to be done. It can be mind-boggling.

Over thirteen moves I learned biblical principles and practical actions that not only helped me let go and start over, but also moved me closer to Christ. I'll be sharing these valuable insights with you in this book, along with the three-step process I used not only to survive, but to thrive through transition. If it helped me, it can help you as well. Those three steps are:

1. Let go
2. Start over
3. Move forward

Let go. The first step in my journey of surviving a move was to *choose to let go.* I had to make the choice to cherish, rather than cling, to anything or anyone that would prevent me from starting over and moving forward with my life.

I needed to be prepared to let go of anything but never to let go of His hand.

I had to let God *mend* any feelings or emotions that kept me from being the whole, happy, and contented woman He wanted me to be.

I had to choose to be open to God's love. So many times when we had moved, my spirit had been closed because of the anger, depression, grief, stress, expectations, comparisons, or discontentment (just to name a few) that I felt. Until I learned to understand my feelings and to go through the process of letting go, I couldn't be open to receive God's love and healing. I couldn't really begin the process of starting over. This time, I knew there was plenty of healing that needed to take place in my heart, and I was ready to let God take control.

Start over. I also had to *choose to start over.* I had to let God *mold* me through this process. As part of starting over, I needed to work through the feelings of loneliness, loss of identity, and inadequacy that threatened to overcome me at times. On the home front, I had to create a new nest all over again, recognize the effects that moving had on our children, and remember the importance of staying connected in my marriage. Of course, I had to be ready for the challenges and opportunities that new beginnings bring to each of us.

Until I allowed God to refine me and teach me through the process of starting over, I couldn't be ready to move forward with my life.

Move forward. Finally, I had to *choose to move forward.* Notice I always use the word *choose.* It is my choice to be open or closed to change and to what God is teaching me through it. I realized it was time to take the focus off myself, embrace where I now lived, and invest in new relationships. It was time to come full circle by being content in my circumstances and choosing to move to a place of peace, joy, hope, and trust, with God as my focus.

I couldn't mature in Christ until I let Him mend and mold me.

I couldn't move forward with my life until I was willing to let go and start over. As I persevered in my walk with Christ, I felt the fulfillment and contentment that only He could bring into my life.

As I began to:
let go
start over
move forward

God began to:
mend
mold
mature

The journey of surviving a move requires action and choice, according to God's plan. I let go—God mends me. I start over—God molds me. I move forward—God matures me.

Take My Hand

Enough about me. I want to talk to you—the uprooted woman, the wounded traveler. This book is written for you, my friend. I have walked in your shoes, felt your joy in the good moves and your pain in the bad ones. God has put you on my heart. He has taken me down the road of thirteen moves to be able to turn around, reach out to you, and take your hand in mine.

Perhaps you've just moved. Maybe you're getting ready to move. Maybe you're dreading it, or maybe you're looking forward to it. My prayer is that this book will help you move closer to God as you begin the journey of letting go, starting over, and moving forward with your life.

I will take you through the process step-by-step. We'll laugh and cry together, but most of all, we'll grow together. Remember, you are not alone! Take my hand, and I'll tell you the rest of the story as we walk the journey together.

"Now glory be to God, who by his mighty power at work within us is able to do far more than we would ever dare to ask or even dream of" (Ephesians 3:20, TLB).

CHAPTER 2

LOOKING BACK

Like a shepherd's tent my dwelling is pulled up and removed from me.
ISAIAH 38:12

"I FEEL SO DETACHED from everyone." Mary Jane was telling me how her move was affecting her.

"My entire root system of family and friends is gone!" she continued. "I feel like a plant that has been pulled from fertile soil, then left to shrivel up and die. Feeling uprooted is overwhelming me. I just want to be put back in my familiar place, surrounded with the same people, and left there to grow!" Her eyes were filled with emotion. Mary Jane had left behind her mom, dad, two sisters and their families, a small business she owned, and an abundance of friends. This was her first move and she was devastated.

What Mary Jane left behind had an enormous effect on her ability to adjust and start over in a new place. When I met her, she had just arrived in Phoenix, and as she put it, she "just couldn't get a grip." She even looked like a withered flower. Her shoulders drooped, she looked pale, and when I hugged her, her body was limp. It was obvious this young woman needed lots of hugs and someone who understood her loss. Mary Jane was grieving for all she had left behind.

When I explained what was happening to her, she asked, "You mean what I feel is normal? I'm really not weird or crazy?" I assured her she was not weird or crazy and that she was going through a grieving process much like what we go through with any major loss.

Here are the steps of grieving that movers can experience:

Denial. Mary Jane refused to accept that Phoenix was her new home. She made no attempt to make new friends or do the obvious things that claim residency, such as getting an Arizona driver's license or Arizona plates for the car.

Anger. Deep down she was angry with her husband and blamed him for taking her away from her family, friends, and successful business.

Depression and sadness. Reality had set in, which was why Mary Jane fit the description of an uprooted, withered flower. She realized this move was for real, and she wasn't going to get to go home tomorrow.

Acceptance. Mary Jane could not start putting her roots down until she accepted her circumstances. She needed to be willing to leave the past behind and start over for the future.

In her book *Women and Their Emotions*, Miriam Neff explains, "Grief is experienced when we must adapt to separation from any person who is important to us, or to an extreme change that has been a meaningful part of our life."[1]

Neff says that grief is a process rather than a series of stages. How true this is in the case of moving! No one can set a time frame for how long it will take to go through the process of grieving and adjusting. Everyone responds differently. For some women it takes weeks, for some months; for some it can take years. Sadly enough, some never make the transition.

Neff also points out that it's not time itself that is the healer, but rather what happens during that time. I have seen women successfully start over by making every effort to do so, and I've seen women become stuck in their own grief and misery.

How much significance you place on what you left behind, and how you have faced change in the past, will play a big part in how well you adjust and adapt.

I wanted to help Mary Jane understand what she was going through. With my arms around her, I said, "Mary Jane, it's all right to cry. Everything and everyone you left behind is worth every tear. Your tears are a part of your healing right now, and you shouldn't keep them bottled up inside." And cry she did. It was as if she needed permission to open the floodgates. It was a healthy release for her.

When the tears subsided, I went on. "Mary Jane, I want you to remember you are not alone here. You may feel cut off from your family and your friends, but you are not cut off from God. He didn't bring you here to abandon you." Just hearing those words seemed to give her new assurance, and I spent the rest of the afternoon helping her to put life in perspective. I wanted her to know that, even though God can do great things in our moving process, there would be emotional lows that are a normal part of letting go. Mary Jane began to understand that the feelings of numbness, emptiness, and sadness were all a part of the loss she felt. I went over again the vital things she needed to remember:

- You are not weird or crazy.
- You will go through a grieving process.
- It's okay to cry.
- You are not alone.

It was important for Mary Jane to know that God has much to say to those of us who pull up stakes and move. I shared with her two of my favorite verses for movers:

"'For I know the plans that I have for you,' declares the LORD, 'plans for welfare and not for calamity to give you a future and a hope'" (Jeremiah 29:11).

"Don't be afraid, for the Lord will go before you and will be with you; he will not fail nor forsake you" (Deuteronomy 31:8, TLB).

I also gave her the verse that had been most dear to my heart during our move to Phoenix, and I'll share it with you again to claim as your moving verse:

"Do not call to mind the former things, or ponder things of the past. Behold, I will do something new, now it will spring forth; will you not be aware of it? I will even make a roadway in the wilderness, rivers in the desert" (Isaiah 43:18-19).

Don't get stuck in past circumstances or hurts. God is going to do new things beyond what you can imagine. Look again, with eyes of faith.

He will make a way for you in this unfamiliar place and transform your desert of disappointments into rivers of renewal.

Remember: With God, there is hope for the future, regardless of the past.

Heart to Heart

Can we have a good heart-to-heart for a minute? That's when I just talk in a down-to-earth way with you. Throughout this book we're going to have a lot of talks like this!

When we moved from Decatur, Georgia, to Raleigh, North Carolina, I left behind my dream house. It was a time in our lives when we were still chasing rainbows. We were excited about Bill's promotion and what it would mean for his career. But I didn't want to leave. The end of my rainbow was in Georgia with a house I loved and that I felt loved me back. That house and I seemed to be in perfect harmony. The more of myself I put into the house and yard, the more joy and contentment it seemed to give me in return.

It was a three-level house built on the side of a hill, with a brook flowing through the backyard. The living room had a sixteen-foot ceiling with glass windows from top to bottom overlooking the woods. What memories we had of that home!

The hotel Bill was managing at the time had a twelve-foot palm tree they were going to get rid of because it looked so puny. Ahhhh, the perfect accessory for a house with a sixteen-foot ceiling. I gave it a new home, named it Percy the Palm Tree, and nursed it back to health. We even had friends who were married in that house under the palm tree.

As we drove away from Decatur, all I could see in the rearview mirror was that wonderful house. It had become my security and my identity. It was the place where I belonged. I didn't care about finding another house in Raleigh. I knew nothing else would ever come as close to being "me."

We looked and looked for the "right" house in Raleigh—in the "right" school district, the "right" neighborhood, and for the "right" price! We found all the "rights" by building our house. I had the opportunity to pick out colors, carpet, and tile to make the new house as close to being me as possible. It helped. No, I couldn't fit a twelve-foot palm tree in the living room, and no, it wasn't as large as the one I'd left behind, but it had a great deck that overlooked the woods.

I learned a lot about myself and about houses from that move. In fact, God has taught me something important through every move, every house, and every place we've lived.

Have you ever stopped to ask yourself, "What is God trying to teach me through all of this?"

These are some of the things God taught me:

- Security does not come from a house (or any other thing, for that matter).
- Real security comes only from trusting in God.
- A house can only bring you happiness; it can't make you happy.
- To grow as a person you need to move beyond your comfort zone.
- Spiritual growth comes in learning to depend on God to meet your needs.
- People, places, and things should not be held too tightly. They can keep you from embracing what God has planned for you.

Someone said a car's windshield is large and the rearview mirror is small because our past is not as important as our future. I'd like to rephrase that to say it's what we do with our past that's important and will have an impact on our future.

When you look in the rearview mirror, what do you see? In the process of letting go, you must first deal with what and whom you left behind, because it will affect your ability to start over. As you look back, you probably see your family, those dear friends, a house and neighborhood you loved, a great job, a church where you worshiped, and a city you called home.

In her book *The Trauma of Moving*, Audrey McCollum writes, "Leaving behind a broken rocking chair in which the first-born was soothed to sleep, a piano around which there was caroling at Christmas, a rusty tricycle—whatever embodies special memories and experiences—can feel like an amputation. It is the loss of a segment of family continuity, of personal history, the loss of a fragment of self." [2]

As women, we have an overwhelming need for a sense of belonging, a sense of community.

That feeling of attachment to someone or something is often lost in the transition of a move. The pain of separation and the reality of being rootless often leave us feeling wounded, affecting our ability to start over.

Never Say Never!

I can hear Abraham saying, "Sarah, God has told me to leave here and move to another country. I don't know where we're going. I only know He's commanded this and I must obey." (See Genesis 12:1.) I'm sure Sarah's response to that kind of news was complete shock. "Do what, Abraham? Go where? How far? How long will it take?" She had never thought about moving! Abraham was successful in his home city of Ur. They had a nice home and financial security. They had deep roots in family and friends.

Can you imagine the questions and feelings that probably went through Sarah's mind? *But Abraham, what about our home? What about our friends? I don't know if I can leave this place where I've lived for so long.*

We've been in this home since we were married. I grew up here, and now you want to take me away to a place I know nothing about, with no idea of where we're going to live or how we're going to get there!

I can only begin to imagine the clutched feeling in her heart. I can see her having a tent sale and selling everything that couldn't fit in a pack carried by a camel. I envision her giving her fine silk garments to friends and cherished heirlooms to family members. She likely gave flowers and vegetables from her garden to her neighbors. Their family and friends probably gave them a farewell party. I'm sure there were laughter and tears and lots of hugs; and then Sarah and Abraham were gone, swallowed up in a cloud of dust from their caravan. Sarah left behind much that had been her security.

I can almost feel Sarah's heart wrenching as she left her beloved home for an unknown place. She went with Abraham out of love, commitment, and obedience; but I know she must have been torn emotionally between staying and leaving, as many of us have been at some time.

Like us, I'm sure Sarah also learned a lot about herself from that move. I know she discovered that her security came from trusting God for what would lie ahead, not in what she left behind. She found that God moved her from her place of comfort to a place of spiritual growth. She learned not to hold on to things too tightly in order to embrace what God had planned for her.

Sarah and I, like many other women who have moved, have learned the wisdom of "Never say never!" In His time, God showed both Sarah and me His plans. Sarah gave birth to a child she thought she would never have, and I got to move back to Georgia!

Learn from Those Who Have Gone Before You

I always like to share Abraham and Sarah's story with women who have moved or are moving. They are our "moving mentors." Not only can we identify with Sarah, but by observing Abraham, we can learn valuable lessons that will equip us for any journey. The Lord had said to Abraham, "Go forth from your country, and from your relatives and from your father's house, to the land which I will show you" (Genesis 12:1). "And he went out, not knowing where he was going" (Hebrews 11:8).

By faith, Abraham obeyed God and set out on a thousand-mile journey through a hostile environment to an unknown land, with nothing but a promise awaiting him at the end of the trip.

He demonstrated his faith in God by moving.

He experienced detours, disagreements, and discouragement along the way. Through it all, Abraham held on to his faith and the promises of God.

What step of obedience and act of faith is God calling you to take?

Abraham responded to God's command, and he learned from the experience. God took Abraham on a journey of obedience, faith, trust, and hope.

Obedience. Abraham didn't *react* to going; he *responded* to going. He didn't react by getting upset, arguing, and being negative. His response was to obey and just do it! Abraham sought to do God's will, not his own will. When you really don't want to go, it's so difficult to respond with a positive attitude and with enthusiasm when the transfer comes or the new job means relocating.

But it is a choice we make—a choice to rebel or obey, to walk *with* God or walk *away* from God.

Faith. Abraham's faith was in the promises of God and in knowing that God would fulfill His promise. It takes a lot of faith to face the unknown. But what a comfort it is to know that God promises not to leave us or forsake us. (See Deuteronomy 31:8.) My faith is wrapped around God's promises in Scripture. I've traveled down many roads reciting my favorite Scripture verses and holding on to nothing more than God's promises.

Trust for provision. Abraham knew God would cover all the details if he would simply trust Him. When our house in Georgia didn't sell, I had to trust that God was in control. When nothing went according to plan, I had to trust that God had everything figured out. I had to have faith that God was working through all the details of all my moves.

It's in that moment of complete surrender and trust, when you truly let go and let God take over, that your life takes a new direction.

Hope for the future. Abraham had great hope for tomorrow and for

God's plan to be fulfilled. With each move, my heart held new hope—hope for our future, our dreams, our plans. That hope became part of my persevering spirit. I know it's hard to leave everything behind and move to a place that is unknown. But never lose hope in what God is capable of doing through this transition in your life.

These principles from the lives of Sarah and Abraham are timeless. When they are applied to your own life, they will equip you for any journey you will ever encounter.

Unpack Your Survival Box

Mary Jane, my moving friend you met at the beginning of this chapter, asked me for some practical suggestions to help her adjust to her new life and community. This is what I gave her and will be giving you in several of the chapters ahead—a survival box of ideas to make your transition easier.

- Keep a journal. Putting your thoughts and feelings on paper will be healing for you. Months from now, it will be good to look back and see where you were and the progress you've made toward settling in.
- Don't procrastinate; get those boxes unpacked!
- Plant flowers, bulbs, or seeds to remind yourself that you are putting down roots to grow here.
- Learn the history of the new town, city, or state you now live in so you can begin to appreciate the place where you live.
- Dwell on the positive and not the negative.
- Find a new church. When you have found one, you are home.
- Consider investing in your community by volunteering at a local charity, a library, a hospital, or being a guide at a local museum or city event.
- If you love to read, join a book club. Check your local bookstore or library for an existing book discussion group.
- Make a goal each week of learning about one new restaurant, place of interest, or shop.

- If there is a local YMCA, community center, dog park, or recreational park in your area, GO! It could be a wonderful way to meet people.
- If you feel like you haven't made a connection in your new home or city yet, don't give up. Remember, tomorrow is another day, and in God's perfect timing, you'll hear yourself saying, "At last I'm beginning to put down some roots."

Do you *cherish* or do you *cling to* what was left behind? Let's move on to the next chapter and find the answer.

CHAPTER 3

CHERISH OR CLING?

Though time and miles may separate us, I have built a
bridge of lovely memories to span the distance.
VIRGINIA TUBBS

I CHERISH THE CARD that a friend from Atlanta sent me with the above quote printed on it. I keep it in my memory box, along with other special cards and notes I've received when we've moved. I even had it framed and kept it on my kitchen counter the first few years we were here in Phoenix, as a reminder of all the precious memories, family, and friends we left behind in Georgia, Florida, North Carolina, and South Carolina.

I have a black-and-white picture of me with my two close friends taken years ago in Atlanta—we called ourselves the Three Musketeers. There we are, posing with our look-alike hairdos parted down the middle. It sits on my desk along with other pictures of the three of us taken over the years. The pictures and the framed quote are reminders of how long we've been friends. Neither time nor miles has diminished our devotion and love for each other. I have cherished these two women as friends and sisters in Christ for over thirty years; yet for most of those years we've been separated. We are proof that a cherished friendship never dies.

I also left behind beloved mentors to both Bill and me, and I am still mentored through their love and devotion. We left behind a wonderful schoolteacher who taught both our children and then became a dear family friend. She continued to influence them long after they were grown. I cherish all of their friendships and yet we live two thousand miles apart.

I left behind my close immediate family when we left Fort Walton Beach, Florida. I cherish the imprint they've made on my life. An artist draws a subject on canvas to give it substance and form, then paints it to give color and life. Daddy gave me substance and form, and Mama gave me color and a love for life.

I cherish the memories of our family gatherings around the dining room table. Mama celebrated every occasion, every holiday, and always had themed decorations for the table. I treasure the view of the Destin Bridge with its shades of blue water from the Gulf of Mexico gleaming underneath. I fondly remember the wild sea oats that grew nestled in the sand dunes on the "world's most beautiful beaches."

I cherish my South Carolina heritage—magnolias, oak trees, barbecues, family reunions, the "low country," hammocks, front porches, and fried chicken. All these remembrances are like buds, ready to blossom at any moment into a bouquet of lovely memories. I cherish what I've left behind. It permeates my life with a fragrance that is identified with who I am.

Release Your Grip on the Past

I have often looked back and thought, *What if I had chosen to cling to the past rather than cherish it? What if I had chosen not to let go? Could I ever really have started over in all our moves?*

Dianna lived in Arizona practically her whole life before moving to Minnesota. I spent time with her before she left, trying to prepare her for the road ahead. She later wrote to me from Minnesota and said, "I'm not very good at letting go. I kept remembering that you said I needed to, but I kept resisting. Now I understand what you were telling me. I see how holding on to everything in Phoenix keeps me from starting over here. Finding things to thank God for in my new place helps me focus on the present, not the past. And another thing that helps, ironically enough, is going back home. It helps me let go. When I go back, it makes me realize that even though I'll always love my family, my life isn't there anymore."

Heart to Heart

Let me share some insight with you as we have a little heart-to-heart together. The more I thought about cherishing and clinging, the more I asked myself the question: *What should we cherish, and what should we cling to?* I'm a visual person and it helps when someone shows me, simply and clearly, the differences between two ideas. Perhaps you've never really understood these two words and the difference they make in your adjustment after a move.

To cherish means "to hold in the mind, to treasure, to hold dear, to value highly." *To cling* means "to clutch, to cleave, to hold on to, to grab hold of." Let's apply those definitions to moving.

- Cherish what was.
- Cling to what is and to what never changes.
- Cherish what you left behind.
- Cling to what you brought with you.

The following are examples:

CHERISH	CLING TO
Family you left behind	Our unchanging God
Friends you left behind	God's truth
Memories that you treasure	God's promises
The job you left behind	Your Bible
The house you loved	Your faith

CHERISH	CLING TO
The church you loved	Hope
Your heritage, your roots	Prayer
The city/town you left behind	Each other
	Your values
	The positive, not the negative

What are you holding on to that is keeping you from moving forward? You owe it to yourself, your husband, and your children to begin the process of letting go. You must discern between what to cherish and what to cling to.

I'm not saying any of this is easy. It reminds me of times when I'm in the ocean, trying to swim to shore with the waves, only to find that the undercurrent pulls me back out again. It's a constant struggle trying to go forward and then being pulled back into the sea. The only time I make it to shore without being swept back is when I stand up and walk forward with determination. Sometimes the only way we can stop from being washed back into a sea of memories is to stand firm, walk forward, and not allow anything to pull us backward or take us under. The force of the current is still there, but we choose to move away from its undertow.

A Contented Penguin

Allicia moved ten times. Her last move was from California to Florida. She shared with me how hard it was for her to connect with others after so many moves. "I hesitated at first to connect because leaving friends is like having a favorite pet that gets run over—you just hate to replace it because you know the new one could get run over too."

She went on to say, "I noticed a pattern in my moving. The places that were the most meaningful to me were the ones where I needed God the most. They were also the ones where I prayed the most. The more intimate I was with God, the more time I spent with Him, the more I grew. I began to put my expectations not in a place, but in a Person. Because my places have changed and will again, I must fasten my heart on something else, for where my treasure is, that's where you'll find my heart. My heart must be stabilized in God, who is unchanging."

I love what she said next: "On my refrigerator is a verse from Philippians 4:11, 'I have learned to be content in whatever circumstances (state) I am.' Below that is a picture of a penguin on a tropical island under an umbrella, sitting on a large ice cube sipping tea, with the words: 'For I have learned in whatever *state* I am, to be content!' Contentment is the result of much prayer. It produces a peace within me and then within my husband and my children."

Allicia is an example of a woman who has learned to *cling* to God and to prayer in her moves.

Across the Miles

Cherish the past, recognizing that God will single out relationships that will endure, no matter the time between visits and the miles between you. Lasting friends are like cream that rises to the top. Your acquaintances may be many, but cherished friends will rise up to stay in your heart forever. The following ideas describe simple things you can do for family and friends to deepen and enrich relationships across the miles:

Remember birthdays. Remember, it's the thought that counts! Mailing a gift can get expensive, so be creative and try my "birthday-party-in-a-card" idea! I keep balloons, confetti, birthday banners (they come in a crepe paper roll—just tear off a few "Happy Birthdays"), streamers, napkins, and other birthday supplies on hand. A balloon, some confetti, a birthday banner, a few streamers, and a napkin will all fit neatly into an envelope. I write on the card, "Since I can't be there, I'm sending you a party in a card!"

There are some other small remembrances that will fit in a card: bookmarks, hankies, tea bags, a packet of seeds, a pressed flower, or a gift card—to name a few. Don't forget books and stationery; CDs and DVDs are great to mail, and they fit right inside a mailing envelope.

Remember Christmas. Send newsletters, magazine subscriptions (we sent *Arizona Highways* to our family so they could learn about the state), framed pictures, or an ornament related to your locale. Over the years, I have mailed little ceramic cacti, plastic chili peppers, and a tin cowboy boot. It sounds hokey, but they looked cute on our friends' trees! Don't forget other special occasions too.

Plan the timing of your phone calls. Don't forget the time changes nationally and internationally. Many times we've called and accidentally awakened family and friends at one or two in the morning!

Make a prayer calendar with names of friends, family, and children on each day of the month. Put their state or city underneath their names. Don't forget to include yourself! You can do this online and send it to everyone. What a great reminder to pray on a certain day of the month for a special person and to know others are praying for you.

Plan visits so you'll always have something to look forward to. It's comforting to know there is a certain time set aside and a commitment made for a visit. Our friends would always plan to visit us in April when the desert is in bloom, and we would go home for the Fourth of July for family reunions and beach time.

Be creative in ways that span the miles. The first year we were in Phoenix, I wanted to send my close friend something that would remind her we would always be connected. I went to a boutique and met a lady who customized words on signs. I asked her to create "The Arizona-Georgia Connection" as a visual reminder of our friendship across the miles. You might want to check online for creative ideas.

Try some of these suggestions. They will ease your transition and help you to cherish those you left behind.

The Flying Trapeze

Until you let go of the past and begin to cherish it (hold in mind, treasure, hold dear), you can't start over and cling to (cleave, hold on to, grab hold of) the present and move forward to embrace the future.

In Paul Tournier's book *A Place for You*, he gives a wonderful illustration of letting go that I have shared with many women and want to pass on to you:

I thought of the trapeze artists, swinging on their trapezes high up under the dome of the circus tent. They let go of one trapeze just at the right moment, to hover for a moment in the void before catching hold of the other trapeze. As you watch, you identify yourself with them and experience the anxiety of the middle-of-the-way, when they have let go of their first support and have not yet seized the second support. What is the force that holds people back, what prevents them from letting go? It is the middle-of-the-way anxiety. It is the void in which they are going to find themselves before being able to seize a new support.

All this to say, we must always be letting go: leaving one place to find another, leaving one support to reach the next, turning our backs on the past in order to thrust wholeheartedly toward the future.[1]

When I read Tournier, it brought back vivid memories of going to the circus as a child. I remember the times when two trapeze artists would catch on to the same bar and, with hands clasped together, swing toward the other trapeze. Then they'd release the one they were holding and almost instantly catch the new one. They always worked in twos or threes, swinging together, hand in hand. Sometimes one person waited at the new bar, ready to reach out and grasp the hands of the trapeze artist, while another stayed behind to help push off.

But underneath there was always a safety net! If someone fell, he or she quickly bounced back up and kept on going.

Do you see what I see?

God is the one who clasps your hand as you move from one place to another.

He is the one who has gone ahead of you, prepared a place for you, and will hold out His hand for you to cling to when you feel alone.

He was with you when you started and will be with you when you finish.

If you should fall along the way, He will be there to protect and guide you and make sure you keep going.

He is your safety net.
Thank You, God, for this blessed assurance to all who move!

Walk in Their Shoes

Once again I am reminded of ordinary people in the Bible who were directed by God to go on extraordinary journeys. They chose to cling to God and His promises, armed with their faith, hope, and prayer. Can you find yourself in any of their stories?

Noah. He lived out his trust in God by picking up a hammer and a saw and building a boat. It's one thing to travel over land, but over water—for 150 days? (I wonder if anyone got seasick on the trip.)

God didn't send Noah into the middle of a flood and then forget about him. He hasn't brought you to this point in your life to abandon you either. God remembered Noah, and He remembers you. (See Genesis, chapters 6-9.)

God will not send you where He cannot sustain you.

Abraham. I'm sure his story resonates with many movers today: the unexpected call to leave behind everything. Just pick up and go, no questions asked. (I think I would have dug my heels in the sand.)

Abraham obeyed when he didn't know *where* (see Hebrews 11:8-10), *how* (vv.11-12), *when* (vv. 13-16), or *why* (vv.17-19). The life of Abraham is an example for all of us to walk by faith. (See Genesis, chapters 12-25.)

Do you walk by faith or by sight?

Moses. He was being prepared for important work by spending forty years waiting and tending sheep. God sent him from his home— his comfort zone—to lead the Israelites out of Egypt to the Promised Land. It was the presence of the Lord that gave Moses the strength and confidence he needed as he led the people of Israel during their wilderness wandering for forty years. (What a trip that was!) He persevered because the Lord was with him and he relied on God's promises. (See Exodus and Deuteronomy.)

Perhaps God is preparing you for something pretty awesome, too, and has used this move to take you out of your comfort zone.

Paul. Paul was one of the greatest missionaries of all times as he traveled from town to town proclaiming the gospel. He was also a man of great courage and hope. He never gave up, though he suffered persecution and imprisonment on land and sea. (See Acts, beginning in chapter 9.)

Don't ever give up or lose heart in the worst of times.

Joseph. His journey through tough family issues, betrayal, enslavement, and imprisonment seemed so unfair. Though he must have felt like a victim of circumstances, his trust in God didn't waver. Through it all, God watched over Joseph and brought good out of evil and difficult situations. God was preparing Joseph for bigger things—like being the ruler of Egypt. Most people would have given up, but because Joseph was faithful in the small things, God raised him up to greater things. (See Genesis, chapters 37-40.)

Don't lose hope. God doesn't waste your trials in life. He will redeem what you are going through.

No matter where you've been, where you are, or where you are going, knowing Jesus Christ can change the course of your life. For these people, their journey, or move, provided an opportunity to establish a deeper walk with God. They had unlimited opportunities to trust Him, to depend on Him, and to cling to Him. Take some time to read in depth about these patriarchs of our faith whose lives were a testimony of clinging to God.

What opportunity to trust God does your move provide?

Marian, a moving friend who lives in Colorado, says it so well, "Realize that God places us where we are to prepare us for what He wants us to become." Never forget, the road has been traveled before you.

The choice to cherish the past and cling to God for the future is not always easy, but faith, hope, perseverance, prayer, and obedience pave the road ahead.

"I do not regard myself as having laid hold of it yet; but one thing I do: forgetting what lies behind and reaching forward to what lies ahead, I press on toward the goal for the prize of the upward call of God in Christ Jesus" (Philippians 3:13-14).

Unpack Your Survival Box

Here are some things to remember, and to do, as you begin to cherish the past and cling to God:

- Don't expect things to be the same in your new location as they were in the old one. This usually ends in disappointment.
- Focus on what you have here, not on what you had there. Accept being where you are.
- Let go of expectations that you'll move back.
- Share with friends and family what's unique about your new town. E-mail or text a picture of something or some place that represents that unique quality.
- Send something small to a close friend that you have cherished as a memento or keepsake.
- Write your loved ones and tell them how much you cherish them in your life. Written words are treasures to keep.
- Subscribe to a magazine or local newspaper from back home as a reminder of the past. I still cherish *Southern Living*!
- Take a picture of you or your family holding a sign that reads, "We love you. Remember us. We cherish you." Or include your own meaningful message. Text or e-mail it to family and friends.
- Make a "home tour" video on your phone to send to family and friends. Include the house, yard, kids, dog, new neighborhood, the kids' new friends, schools, church, and anything else that says, "This is my new life here!"
- Don't constantly think about what you're leaving behind, but rather what you have to look forward to in the future.
- Tell yourself there's never a place you want to stay if God wants you somewhere else. The best place to be is where God wants you to be.

In the next chapter, we are going to talk about some important initials, MSM, and their big impact on your move!

CHAPTER 4

THE STRESS OF MOVING

Be strong and courageous! Do not tremble or be dismayed,
for the LORD your God is with you wherever you go.
JOSHUA 1:9

"I AM GOING TO EXPLODE!" Ann said as she raised her voice above those of the other women in the room. You could have heard a pin drop as silence fell over the room and all eyes turned to Ann. About twenty newcomers were gathered for a weekly Moving On After Moving In study at our church. (Moving On After Moving In is a multisession study available at Just Moved Ministry, www.JustMoved.org.)

"I feel like someone lit my fuse six months ago when Jim told me we were going to move; we've been here for one month now, and my fuse is getting shorter and shorter!"

Ann's voice was beginning to break with emotion and you could feel the empathy rise in the room. Some of the women had been there; others were feeling the same turbulence within themselves. "What's happening to me?" Her eyes pleaded as she spoke. "I feel like I'm going to jump out of my skin! My life has been turned upside down, I'm exhausted, and there are still boxes that haven't been unpacked. I can't find things I need in the house, not to mention the grocery store. I yell at the kids for no reason, and my husband is too busy to help me hang the curtains."

Someone laughed and broke the ice by saying, "Welcome to the MSM world of newcomers! You've got what we refer to as Moving Stress Meltdown! It comes from the stress overload factors that moving creates."

Ann smiled slightly and asked, "What in the world is that, and is there a cure?"

I spoke up and said, "Oh yes! There's a cure all right. Time is a big influence, but there are lots of other things that can help you too. First of all, though, let me explain what we mean by Moving Stress Meltdown.

"Since there are labels and names for everything these days, it just seemed natural that we should have our own term for what we go through when we move. No one really seems to acknowledge that the trauma and transition of moving is serious. It's like a closet illness. The stress that movers go through has been hidden away for too long. Yet it affects every area of our lives, often leaving us devastated.

"Our lives are like a puzzle that's been turned upside down, and we have to somehow put all the pieces back together in order.

"We thought it would be healthy and fun for all women who go through the same thing when they move, to have a name for what they're going through. It breaks the ice and makes us laugh!"

MSM was a new insight for Ann, and it's helpful for all of us who are willing to acknowledge the stress that is unique to us as movers.

The Overload Factors in Moving

As we continued to talk, I said, "Ann, let me tell you what the stress overload factors in moving are. I think it will help you understand why you feel you're going to explode."

I explained to her that anything that exceeds our normal stress level can throw us into overload very quickly. (We all have a stress level that varies depending on the circumstances of our lives.) People are like washing machines that get out of balance when too many clothes pile up on one side. Unbalanced wash loads make terrible noises and threaten to shake their way across the floor. To avoid that, we have to stop the washing machine, redistribute the clothes or take some out, then start it again.

It is the same way with us. When we are on stress overload, we have to stop, balance our physical or emotional load or eliminate some of it, and start again. From the moment we find out we are going to move, whether we're happy or sad about it, our stress level will rise. The anticipation, preparation, and implementation take us off the routine path of life and set us up for stress. Our minds start anticipating the changes to come. Our to-do list becomes overwhelming. All this happens before we even begin moving. We still don't know what to expect when we get to our destination.

Many of us have people who will help with the physical move, but few of us have anyone to help with the emotional move. Even under the best circumstances, emotional stress is inevitable. Moving puts us on the overload cycle.

Stress overload factors fall into these three categories:

Packing and unpacking. You're not just packing and unpacking your belongings; you're packing and unpacking your *life*. The physical labor alone is exhausting, but you're also experiencing emotional exhaustion as you relive the memories attached to your possessions. Then, when something is broken or damaged in the move, it is one more loss.

Instead of looking around at all that needs to be done, try looking up and focusing your eyes on Jesus.

Adjustment to a new location. There are so many little things that can add up quickly and throw you off balance. Just finding answers to these questions is stressful: When is mail delivered? When is garbage pickup? Where's the best grocery store, bank, doctor, service person, or mechanic?

Instead of thinking about all the things you don't know about your new community, think about what you do know—God is here, in this place!

Destructive comparisons. We compare everything: the weather was better back home, the traffic wasn't as bad, the people were friendlier. We tend to remember the good about where we used to live more than the bad. *Everything* appears better than it truly was. It usually takes about a year to balance out the comparisons.

Instead of comparing what was, think about the positive of what is.

Stress can show up in a physical manner also. Know your own body and watch for weight gain or loss, insomnia, backaches, headaches, and other physical symptoms. It can also show up in emotional highs and lows. Watch for signs and seek help before they become severe. Take care of your body! The last thing you want are physical ailments in addition to your emotional stress.

C-H-A-N-G-E—Small Word, Big Impact!

In addition to being on overload from moving, don't overlook the impact that any major life change might have on you. Usually you will try everything to avoid change, because many times it is associated with the pain of giving up something or someone. If you can't avoid it, then you try to manage it to better control the outcome. If you can't manage it, then you try to shortcut it somehow. You think it would be easier if you could just bypass the hard parts. But then you are missing what God is teaching you through the whole process—things you could learn no other way.

It's not what you will do with change—but what God will change in you!

The Case of the Despondent Desert Dwellers

At this point, I can't help but think of the Israelites as they left Egypt to move to Canaan, the Promised Land (see Exodus 13:17-15:21). They thought it would be a pretty quick trip, but it turned out to be a forty-year journey through the desert. Talk about a major life change and being stressed out and on overload—they are a prime example of that for us today.

Can you imagine packing and unpacking for forty years to get to your destination? It would physically wear you out and wear you down, to the point of 24-7 exhaustion. It became really easy to be miserable and unhappy with their situation *when they took their eyes off of God.*

Then, can you imagine the adjustment issues they had—to the *wilderness,* in the *desert,* for that long period of time? Any hardship or discomfort led to so much complaining and whining, they even wanted to go back to Egypt. All this, because *they forgot to follow God's leading.*

And let's not forget how easy it was for the Israelites to compare life in the wilderness with the way they remembered life in Egypt. Everything they left behind appeared better than it was. They remembered the good more than the bad *when they forgot to trust God.*

Okay, let's switch back to now. Here are a few personal and practical stress relievers to keep in mind. Not that the Israelites couldn't have benefited from them too!

- *Rest and relax.* It's a great detox for your mind when you feel overwhelmed.
- *Eliminate and simplify.* Remember, less is more. You don't have to be all and do all at once.
- *Be flexible and forgiving.* It's okay to break routine and not have a tight schedule all the time. It's also good for the soul to forgive others and to ask for forgiveness when you blow your cool under stress.
- *Be grateful and grin.* You'll stress less when you have a grateful heart and show your gratitude with a smile.

(You'll find more ideas as you unpack your survival box.)

You're in Good Company

To help you get the big-picture perspective, remember the US census report showing that over 35.9 million people moved in one year in the US, and 18 million were women.[1] You're in good company! You share a common bond with all these women, and yes, especially the Israelites! You've all suffered in some way or another from MSM.

After Ann exploded in our class, several of the women chimed in to tell her their own moving stories and experiences. It was a comfort to Ann, and these stories may comfort you too.

Dianna boldy stated, "I expected moving to be an adventure, to be lonely and hard, to add hassle and stress to my life, yet to be culturally enriching, to draw us closer as a family, to be a challenge to our marriage, to stretch me spiritually. I was looking forward to the relief of not working, and to being at home with my kids. I knew moving would be hard on my kids growing up so far away from their grandparents. At the same time, I thought it would be exciting to be surrounded by a new culture. Moving was all of that." She had moved twice in less than two years. Then she added, "By the time all the preparations are done, I'm ready to leave. I get tired of saying good-bye. I reach a point where I just want to get it over with. I get nervous, scared, and excited. Then it's such a weird feeling to get off a plane in a new city and think, *I just moved here. This is my new home. I live here now.* It seems like it should take longer and be more difficult than a plane ride."

Dianna went on, "At first, Ann, it's so exciting! I love to buy new things for the house, try out new restaurants, check out the malls, and discover all the new places to go. Then, when all that wears off, it stops being exciting and becomes frustrating. It takes time to adjust and accept all the changes."

Beverly, who had moved nine times, spoke up in a gentle voice. "Realize it will take time to adjust. Things won't be the same, but even though they're different, they may be better. God is faithful. He won't leave us. And we do grow from each new experience."

Sudie, who had moved ten times, said calmly, "Believe it or not, a major stress for me was trying to find the right hairdresser! That's so important to all of us. I'd travel across town for the right haircut. My hair is an expression of who I am, and as it is, I already lose enough of my identity when we move."

Alma, who had moved three times, laughed and said, "The biggest adjustment for me was going from a very busy lifestyle with a full calendar to a calendar with nothing written on it!"

Judy, who had moved ten times, spoke from experience, "I allow myself the freedom to feel the pain of moving. It's difficult. Don't expect too much too soon. I have to make positive choices to begin nesting in the new place. If my feelings get too overwhelming, I take a break and go to a movie. Live today, look for the positive, and don't burden everybody with negatives."

God truly does work in loving ways through His people as they touch the lives of others with compassion, sensitivity, and understanding. When someone has walked in your "movin' shoes," they know the road you've traveled. We all felt good after the women had shared their thoughts and feelings and offered encouragement to Ann. Our morning had given purpose and significance to one more mover.

Running Away from It All

A life change like moving is not easy. But God doesn't always want to make it easy for us, for it's in those stressful times that we grow closer to Him. *Sometimes God allows us to go through an experience for the powerful lessons we could learn no other way.*

I remember a particularly stressful time when we first moved to Phoenix. I ran away from home. To this day, I can't even remember the specific reason; I only remember I felt like a balloon that had been filled beyond capacity and would burst at any moment if the pressure was not released. My release was to leave home.

I got into my unreliable compact car early one morning and proceeded to drive southeast of Phoenix with my eyes fixed on the beautiful Superstition Mountains. They looked like a place of refuge for me, an oasis in the middle of the desert. I rolled the windows down and felt the cool October morning air on my face. I let the wind blow through my hair and let the tears roll down my cheeks as I turned off the main highway toward the mountains.

The sign said "Apache Trail," and I remembered reading something about it being an authentic Indian trail. That sounded adventurous enough, so I kept going. I soon came to a sign that said, "Pavement ends—proceed at your own risk." *Why not?* I thought. I felt daring and unafraid.

The road went higher and higher into the mountains. Then it became a switchback trail, getting rougher and narrower, a mere ledge on the side of the mountain with a tremendous drop to a lake below. It was impossible to turn around. The only way out was to keep going.

About that time the car began to sputter and overheat. I kept turning the key in the starter for fear it would completely die out. I knew if it stalled, I'd be stranded without a phone (no cell phones in that day), no passing cars, and no people in sight. I was in the middle of nowhere. Now, I'm not a fearful person, but the reality of what was happening hit me. I had no control over the situation. I was completely alone and had foolishly put myself in a dangerous predicament. The car could have gone over the side of the trail, down the canyon, and into the lake. It could have stalled. If that had happened, I would have been stranded for who knows how long, and I would have been at the mercy of anyone who might show up on the trail. I was afraid for my life.

All of a sudden, everything came into perspective. Nothing seemed as important as getting to the other side of the mountain so I could go home to Bill and the children. My prayers, God's Word, and songs of praise paved the road I was traveling. I prayed out loud as I clutched the steering wheel. I said my favorite Bible verses over and over. I sang all the old hymns and worship songs I could remember.

My perspective changed from focusing on the stress that my move had caused to focusing on my relationship with God.

Not only did I feel His presence in the car; I actually felt Him in control as the car miraculously kept going.

After two hours on the Apache Trail—two hours of an intense refresher course about who God is in my life—I saw the highway in the distance ahead. It was eighty miles back to Phoenix and I didn't dare stop the car, knowing it wouldn't start again. It was almost dark by the time I sputtered up the driveway and said, "Thank You, Lord, for getting me home safely. I'll never do that again!" (I didn't tell Bill what I had done until much later. It was hard to admit I had been that careless.)

God taught me some powerful lessons that day. For one thing, I haven't done anything that foolish since! The other things I learned are in our Heart to Heart.

What "Apache Trail" have you been on, and what did you learn from the experience?

Into the Unknown

With my imagination, I couldn't help but see a few parallels between my experience and Joshua's experience.

Joshua may not have had an Apache Trail, but he sure entered into unknown territory when he led the people of Israel into the Promised Land. My unknown territory was moving to Phoenix. (I can't say that it was the Promised Land!)

Joshua had to step out in faith to cross over the Jordan River. I had to continue in faith to navigate the Apache Trail.

Joshua's strength and courage came from meditating on the Word of God, believing God's promises, and then moving forward with the assurance of God's presence. My strength and courage came from repeating Scripture verses out loud, praying, singing worship songs, and feeling God's presence with me. That was what I needed to turn my fear to faith and persevere to keep moving forward.

Joshua made it to the other side of the Jordan River and into the new territory. (See Joshua, chapters 1-4.) I made it to the other side of the Apache Trail and headed back to my new territory, Phoenix!

 ## Heart to Heart

"Be strong and courageous! Do not tremble or be dismayed, for the LORD your God is with you wherever you go" (Joshua 1:9). Whatever trail you might be on emotionally after your move, just remember:

Do not tremble. When the road gets rough, slow down, take a deep breath, put things in perspective, and depend upon God to get you through the circumstances. He *will* enable you to make it.

Do not be dismayed. When you can't turn around, focus on God and on what's in front of you. Looking back isn't going to help you get beyond the move. If your focus is on Him, God will equip you with whatever is necessary to move ahead.

The Lord your God is with you wherever you go. When you feel alone and afraid, remember who accompanies you. Turn to God for the comfort of His presence and the calming of your fears. He will embrace you with His Word and protect you with His strength and courage. He is behind you, beside you, and ahead of you.

Be strong and courageous. When your vehicle (your body and emotions) starts to fail you and you realize you're out of control, verbally give God the steering wheel in your life. Depend on Him to get you through this crisis. Let His strength be your strength. He will encourage you and uphold you.

Remember, when you are on overload and stressed out from your move, God will:

> *Enable you*
> *Equip you*
> *Embrace you*
> *Encourage you*

And God's presence is the best GPS road map!

 ## Unpack Your Survival Box

To help you reduce the stress of moving:

- Don't get too upset over broken things. Something always breaks or gets damaged. Remember, they are just things.

- Pick one room and concentrate on getting it settled so you have a place to rest while everything else is in disarray.
- Trust God . . . even when it seems everything is going wrong.
- Join a spin or Zumba class, take a long walk, be intentional about some form of exercise. All are great stress relievers.
- Remember, Rome wasn't built in a day, and your house won't be settled in a day either.
- Pray about everything.
- Have one goal per day. Don't try to get new license plates, a library card, and a driver's license all at once.
- Reward yourself with a special treat such as new nail polish, a movie, or a magazine when you accomplish a dreaded task.
- Treat yourself to an old favorite stress reliever—a hot bath.
- Go to a mall and browse the stores.
- Read a book you've always wanted to read.
- Listen to praise music.
- Read the book of Exodus in the Old Testament. What the Israelites accomplished was so much more complicated and difficult than any of our moves. It will help put your move into perspective!
- If you are worried about a situation, ask yourself what God would want you to do. Let go of what you can't change or what you have no control over.
- The best way to find out what God says about your situation: Search His Word!
- You can always claim Scarlett O'Hara's famous line, "I'll think about that tomorrow!"

Did your move leave you with a "ding" or a "nick"? How quickly will you recover? Let's find out in the next chapter!

CHAPTER 5

A DING OR A NICK?

In Him all things hold together.
COLOSSIANS 1:17

ONE SATURDAY MORNING when Bill was washing the car, he called me over to look at the door on the passenger side. "What happened here?" he asked, as he pointed to an obvious dent in the door.

"I don't know what happened," I replied. "Surely I didn't do that!"

"Well," he said, "looks like somebody put a pretty strong ding in the side of your door. That's not going to be as easy to fix as a nick would have been."

"What do you mean, not as easy to fix?" I asked curiously. "What's the difference between a ding and a nick?" (It felt like a bonding moment with Bill.)

"Well, I'll show you the difference," he said, as we walked to the other side of the car. "This is a nick," he explained as he pointed to it. "It's just a chip and it can be touched up with matching paint. The difference between a ding and a nick is the force of the blow."

"Bill, now it's clear to me!" I said in excitement.

He laughed as he said, "Well, it's not that hard to figure out, Susan!"

"No, no, I mean that's the way it is when you move! A move can be a ding or a nick, depending on the impact."

If a move is a ding, it's going to be harder to repair than if the move is just a surface nick. A ding has to be repaired from the inside. Repair has to come from internal healing or restoration.

The repair should be a lot easier when it is a nick. The impact of a nick can be repaired from the outside. The repair can come from a surface change, like a smile or a hug. It really does depend on the force of the blow.

So I ask you, was your move a ding or a nick?

A Moving Experience

To help you answer that, let me ask you two questions:

Was your move planned or unplanned?

Was your move wanted or unwanted?

I ask these questions to newcomers a lot, because they can give me a quick handle on the movers' situation. Many women and families want to relocate and look forward to moving. It can mean a promotion, a better lifestyle, an opportunity to start over, a chance to live in a different climate, financial and professional advancement, retirement, health benefits, a chance to be near family, or they could just be ready for a change. These people have the opportunity to plan ahead and be prepared. For those who expect a move, there are no surprises.

For those who want the move, it can be a happy experience. It can be anticipated with enthusiasm. But even moving for all the right reasons can lead to disillusionment, disappointment, and unmet expectations. That, in turn, can determine whether your transition is a ding or a nick.

How you start your move is important; how you finish your move is vital—to your well-being and to your family's.

On the other hand, it can make a big difference if the move was unplanned and you had two weeks' notice, or less, to pack up and leave. If it was unexpected and you had no choice in the matter, or if it was unwanted and you had no desire to go—that's another story. A vivid example of an unplanned, unexpected, and unwanted move would be what I have coined as a "crisis move."

When the Crisis Hits

When foreclosure of a home happens because of a job loss, an economic setback, a recession, or a natural disaster—such as a flood, fire, tornado, or hurricane—women and families experience what I call a "crisis move."

In a crisis move, your home leaves you, rather than you leaving your home.

Being painfully uprooted under these circumstances can be both physically and emotionally devastating. You are facing traumatic losses, many of which will be life-changing. With the shock of losing a home, you face the fear of an unknown future and a tangled web of feelings and emotions ranging from shame to guilt to embarrassment to anger or bitterness.

Grieving is the last thing you are thinking about. You go into survival mode, not allowing yourself the time to grieve. The emotional fallout of foreclosure or a devastating disaster leaves the shock of "What happened?" and then, "What will happen now?"

For foreclosure families, the stark reality is that no moving van will be coming for a company transfer, and there is no money to buy another house. Often it results in a lower standard of living, selling your belongings, or leaving them behind. Your husband might feel guilty that he can no longer provide for his family's basic needs. You might become angry that he kept "how bad it was" from you and didn't tell you that you would be losing your home. Trust is broken between the two of you. Your kids are confused and don't understand why the family has to move or why they have to switch schools. It's hard to give your kids the emotional support they need when your own emotional tank is empty. You can't afford to move out of town. You have no choice but to stay and deal with the humiliation.

If you've been through a devastating disaster, it's hard to wrap your mind around seeing your home disappear through tragic events beyond your control. You might be left with nothing but the clothes you wear, or what you could take with you when you had to evacuate or hide in your basement for safety. An overwhelming fear for your life, and for your family, becomes an all-consuming reality. Friends and strangers rally to physically support you in areas of need, but the shock is so great, the emotions so raw, that you seem to just go through the motions day by day.

One crisis move is private, the other is public. Both are painful, leaving behind shattered dreams and broken hearts.

The Steel Magnolias

Women from across the nation have shared their stories about the impact of their moves and how their lives were affected. No one seems to escape the kaleidoscope of emotions that comes with any kind of move. From stay-at-home moms to career women, from pastors' wives to military wives, from corporate wives to professional athletes' wives, from happy movers to crisis movers—all share a common bond when it comes to moving.

They hope their stories will give you greater understanding and insight into your own move. Some of their moves were "dings" and some were "nicks." Some, like crisis moves, were devastating "dings." Try to identify them yourself.

Carol, a young widow with three children, never expected to be *alone at the age of thirty-five.* Her husband had been killed in a car accident. She was left without insurance and with no means of support. Carol had to sell their home and move to another state to be near her parents so they could help with the children. Her move was *unplanned* and *unexpected.* Still grieving, her family uprooted, and her future unknown, Carol said, "God will give me the strength I need to get through this."

Dianna moved from New Jersey. "I was so glad to leave, I even forgot to tell my house good-bye!" They had been expecting *a transfer.* However, the job didn't last long and their house didn't sell. They ended up going back to New Jersey.

Joan's move to Connecticut was not necessarily her first choice, but she was ready for the move, since when *a promotion* had come for her husband, he'd had leave within two weeks. It took her four months to pack their belongings and get everything shipped. Though she was sad to leave her friends and church, she was happy to reunite with her husband and start to settle their house.

Linda is a single mom. After her *divorce*, she wanted to start over, so she moved to Arizona with her two children. She was deeply hurt over the divorce, but she knew she had to keep going. Her first priority was to find a job and a place to live. She knew no one and chose Arizona to get as far away from old memories as possible.

Dot is married to a professional athlete. I call her *a gypsy mover.* She might have to move twice a year if her husband is traded to another team. She lives month to month and year to year, based on her husband's performance in the game. Even though they can afford to buy any house they want, it's still hard to put down roots. When they move, Dot's husband has instant friends on the team, but she often doesn't have a single friend to turn to. She says that, even though they live an affluent lifestyle, she feels alone and anxious about being uprooted so often. "I don't always want the next move, but I always have to expect it," she said.

Joanne and her husband had successful careers in a large city. When he became ill and *had to retire*, they decided to move from the city to the country for a simpler life. "We hadn't planned on moving at this time in our life, but knew we had to make a major change in our lifestyle."

Pam celebrated her fortieth birthday two weeks after they *moved back* to Texas. She said, "I felt too old to start over again!" It was easier when her children were younger; now they were teenagers and that made it harder. She thought it would be exciting to reunite with old friends and familiar territory but was soon disappointed that a lot had changed in the three years they'd been gone.

Tracy has a *husband in the military*, so moving is part of life for her and their young daughter. The couple has moved twice in four years of marriage. Tracy looks forward to new opportunities, new culture, and new friends. However, as a young mom in a new place, she often feels lonely and isolated. "It's always hard when you're new and don't know anyone you can spend time with besides the baby, and don't even know anyone who can babysit."

Laurie, a pastor's wife, had lived in one place for twelve years. She and her husband loved their church, had deep roots in the community, and had just finished remodeling their home. She was expecting their second baby. Then her husband was *called to pastor a church in a small town*. "It was very hard to leave a church and congregation we loved and start building relationships all over again," she said sadly. After a year, Laurie still finds it very hard to make friends in a small town where most residents have lived all their lives. She finds it difficult to break into the circles of families and friends already deeply rooted there. Laurie still struggles with the move.

Elizabeth thought they were living the good life in California. Her husband had a good job and a good income—until the economic crisis hit them personally. He came home early one day and told her the company was downsizing and he had been laid off. Their home went into *foreclosure* and was repossessed by the bank. She knew something was wrong but didn't know what until a foreclosure notice was posted on their door. Her husband felt guilty that he could no longer provide for Elizabeth and their three children. She felt shame and anger because of their situation. They moved into a small apartment. Desperate for work, he went from being a corporate executive to working a minimum-wage job. She went from not working at all to a full-time, night shift position. "I feel like we have to rebuild our marriage, as well as our life," Elizabeth said, "but we have not lost hope."

Beth, a young career woman, had taken her first job after college in Florida. When a *hurricane* hit the area, her condo was destroyed. She lost everything and had no flood insurance. The small business where she worked was also destroyed and never recovered. As a newcomer, she didn't know anyone, so she had to stay in temporary shelter at a school until she could go live with relatives out of state. It took almost a year before Beth could find another job, in another state, and get back on her feet again. She still has nightmares about the wind tearing off her roof as she left her condo. She still prays through the memories of that night.

Barb and her husband, Tony, knew the *fire* was spreading fast and heading their way. "Evacuate now!" were words the couple dreaded to hear. They evacuated to a small town in Arizona, taking only what they could load in their pickup truck. Their two dogs went in first, then whatever they could fit in the back. Days later, when it was safe to return, they drove up to all that was left of their mountain dream home—burned down to the foundation. Devastated but resilient, Barb and Tony began rebuilding their home as soon as they could. "What matters," Barb said, "is that God was with us and we survived."

Until We Meet Again

Karen, her name tag read. She was working at the library the day I went there to do some research on this book. I walked up to her desk, told her I was writing a book for women about moving, and asked if she could assist me. "Moving?" Karen said. "I'll tell you about moving!"

I sat down in the chair next to her desk and prepared to listen. I could tell by her voice that I had exposed a painful subject and that she wanted to talk about it. "Do you mind if I write this down? I might be able to use your experiences in my book." This is Karen's story:

When Karen's husband was transferred to Kentucky, he had to start work there immediately. She stayed behind in Phoenix to sell the house and wait for the children to finish out the school year. In the meantime, she went to work to fill her spare time.

Finally, some six months later, the house sold. Karen handled the closing by herself. She then made all the moving arrangements and did most of the packing. She even drove across the country with the children. Her move to Kentucky turned out to be a disaster. She disliked living there so much and was so unhappy that she eventually left her husband and returned to Phoenix with the children.

She said that by handling everything and becoming so independent during the six months they were separated, she knew she could handle things on her own. She blamed her husband's company for not providing better moving arrangements for the family. (Some companies sell the house so the family can move together.) She blamed the move itself for the ultimate breakup of their marriage.

"You're really writing a book to help women through the moving process?" she asked when she finished her story. "Huh! I could have used something like that to help me when I moved. You know, my husband keeps calling me to come back to Kentucky."

"Oh, really?"

"When you finish that book, do you think you could bring me a copy?"

I smiled. "Of course, I'd love to bring you a copy."

And I walked away knowing God can even use a book about moving to introduce Himself to a woman who needs Him in her life.

Moving Overcomers

No matter where I go, or whom I talk with, it seems everyone has a story about moving to share. In each of the stories you've just read, moving has had a different impact. Some experiences have been nicks, some have been dings, others have been devastating dings beyond comprehension. With the possible exception of Karen, all these women had an unwavering faith, an inner strength, and an enduring perseverance that allowed them to overcome their obstacles in moving. Each one's journey of healing varied according to the impact of the move, but they all eventually began to let go, start over, and move forward with their lives.

Let me tell you, specifically, what makes these women "moving overcomers." Their unwavering faith is in Jesus Christ. Their inner strength comes from Him. Their enduring perseverance is a result of knowing Jesus as their Lord. Their stories are different, but their message is the same. May their journeys as moving overcomers give you hope.

Here are some of their thoughts as they reflected on their journey:

"I rely on God to meet my needs."
"I daily surrender myself and my situation to God."
"I try to look at my circumstances from God's perspective."
"God is my security."
"I spend a lot of time in prayer."
"God's Word sustains me."
"I pray about everything."
"I try to remember that God is in control."
"I walk by faith, not by sight."
"God didn't bring us here to go backward."
"I have to let go and trust God."
"He will not leave me nor forsake me."
"I have learned to seek God when there is no one else."
"God brought us here for a purpose. It's enough for me to
    know that."
"We may have lost everything, but we have each other, and we
    have hope."
"I held on to my dignity and my faith in God."

Hold On to the Rope!

Several years ago, a friend shared with me a wonderful story she had read. I have used it many times to help newcomers hold on after a move has caused a ding or a nick in their lives.

The story is a daughter's loving remembrance of her mother. She tells how her mother would refer to a rope that represented her faith in God, and how she would hold on to that rope during hard times. Her mother said, "I felt like a lone mountain climber stranded on the verge of an abyss with no hope, but with the rope coiled on my shoulder . . . I threw the rope into the void, and it held." She referred to the rope as being woven of thousands of strands threaded with God's goodness, His faithfulness, His Word, and most of all, constant prayer. "Pray without ceasing even when you don't feel like it. Keep weaving that rope," she said.[1]

My friends, I also want you to remember that God "weaves in" His promises, His hope, His everlasting love, and His mercy to strengthen the rope all the more. It cannot be pulled apart. The threads of your life have been woven together into a rope strong enough to carry you. Just remember that when you need it, the rope will hold.

When a friend is moving, I give her a piece of white rope with a pink bow tied around it as a reminder of God's love, and I tell her to always hold on to the rope!

Heart to Heart

As I reflect on the dings and nicks of moving, I know that the same is true in all of life. The impact of change affects all of us in some way or another.

If it's a crushing blow, it will seem impossible to put the pieces of our lives together again, but it can be done. In my own brokenness, I have not been shattered. God has put the pieces of my life back together. It looks different now, but there is wholeness from within.

If it's a minor hit, you know the change will not be as difficult. You will adjust and adapt rather quickly, and all the pieces will fall back into place before you know it. Life will soon regain its normal rhythm.

How well we cope with change—and where we find the strength to let go, the faith to start over, and the perseverance to move forward—has a tremendous effect on how well we recover. Don't let the impact of change cause permanent damage to your life.

Being uprooted by any life change can leave you feeling like you've hit rock bottom. You can either stay there or see God as the rock and foundation upon which to rebuild your life.

Unpack Your Survival Box

Scripture passages for a "ding" or a "nick" type of move:

He is before all things, and in Him all things hold together.
COLOSSIANS 1:17

Trust in the LORD with all your heart and do not lean on your own understanding. In all your ways acknowledge Him, and He will make your paths straight.
PROVERBS 3:5-6

Pray without ceasing.
1 THESSALONIANS 5:17

Delight yourself in the LORD; and He will give you the desires of your heart. Commit your way to the LORD, trust also in Him, and He will do it.
PSALM 37:4-5

And we know that God causes all things to work together for good to those who love God, to those who are called according to His purpose.
ROMANS 8:28

But if we must keep trusting God for something that hasn't happened yet, it teaches us to wait patiently and confidently.
ROMANS 8:25, TLB

Don't be afraid, for I am with you. Don't be discouraged, for I am your God.
ISAIAH 41:10, NLT

Come to Me, all who are weary and heavy-laden, and I will give you rest.
MATTHEW 11:28

Even though the fig trees are all destroyed, and there is neither blossom left nor fruit; though the olive crops all fail, and the fields lie barren; even if the flocks die in the fields and the cattle barns are empty, yet I will rejoice in the Lord.
HABAKKUK 3:17-18, TLB (This is one of my favorites!)

I could go on and on with refreshing Scripture passages. But per-haps these verses will inspire *you* to dig deeper into God's Word. Now let's see what you and a suitcase have in common!

CHAPTER 6

HAVE SUITCASE, WILL MOVE

*I live with this feeling of being just a beat-up suitcase that
got misrouted somewhere.*
LAURIE, *a moving friend*

WE'VE SEEN THAT the first step in letting go is dealing with what we've left behind, learning what to cherish and what to cling to, and understanding how deeply our moves have affected us. Now let's look at how much we have in common with the luggage we carry with us when we move.

Being the people watcher that I am, airports are especially fascinating to me. They became my hangout during the years that Bill traveled so much in business. I accumulated a lot of "frequent shuttling miles" driving Bill back and forth to the airport. One time, I waited at the gate for five hours through one delay after another.

When you're an airport groupie as I was, you begin to make observations and learn a great deal about travelers. I've observed that when people first get off a plane, they move quickly to get their luggage. "Mr. Miller, meet your party in the baggage claim area." Sound familiar? The baggage area seems to be the place where everybody ends up. It's where they wait . . . and wait! It's there that I can take the time to really observe people and gather a first impression.

It's obvious that some of the people standing around are coming home. They are chatting in an animated way with family and friends. For other people, however, this seems to be a new experience. They are entering a new phase of their lives—a new town, new job, new friends. I'm sure everything looks magnified and intimidating.

Others have come in sorrow—perhaps because of a death or an illness. They wear their emotions like a heavy cloak. Some people have a look of obvious anxiety; they are not sure what's ahead for them.

And then there are those who are just happy to have reached their destination. They wanted to come, they looked forward to being there, and now they have finally arrived.

It's not too hard to separate the seasoned travelers from the novices, those who are having a familiar experience from those who are in unfamiliar territory. Those who have traveled a lot look either relaxed or bored. Those who are having a first or even second travel experience look uneasy and a little nervous.

It's the same with those who are moving. If you've done it before, it's not too difficult; but if moving is a new experience, you can count on feeling either anxious, sad, apprehensive, or overwhelmed when you finally reach your destination.

Our Luggage Is a Lot Like Us

I began to watch passengers more closely and noticed how some people even looked like their luggage. Businessmen and -women picked up leather, executive-style suitcases. A matching designer set of luggage was claimed by a couple in matching designer clothes. Golf bags belonged to tanned men wearing knit sport shirts and shorts. And very stylish, well-dressed women, wearing lots of jewelry, pulled fancy luggage wrapped in protective vinyl. A large family, with children of all ages, picked up at least eight well-worn bags in all shapes and sizes, with matching ribbons tied to the handles for identification.

I found myself wondering about all these people. Their luggage certainly identified them from the outside, but I wondered what feelings they carried on the inside, safely hidden from view.

You see, as women on the move, much of our identities can be revealed by how our suitcases look from the outside and from the inside.

What Kind of Mover Are You?

I would never think of throwing away my old suitcase. It's very much a part of my life after all these years. It's a friend, an enemy, a traveling companion, a place where I store feelings and emotions, and a keeper of treasures. You might have one just like it—a cheap mustard-colored vinyl bag with a large, ugly zipper. It's dusty, worn-out, frazzled, frayed, scratched up, bent in, coming apart at the seams, all with a broken zipper! There have been times in our moves when I felt like I looked like my suitcase. I claimed it then as my identity.

What would your suitcase look like? Here are a few I've met:

Covered in labels. She's covered with stickers and tags that say *Fragile, Handle with Care, Damaged, Transfer To, Transferred From, Final Destination.* She's not sure who she is and where she's going. She just knows she's lost a major part of her identity. I'll never forget the pastor's wife who came up to me after I finished speaking to newcomers at a seminar. Her eyes were brimming with tears and she asked if she could talk to me for a moment. There was an urgency in her voice as she said, "We just moved here, and everybody wants a piece of me. Will I teach Sunday school? Will I play the piano? Will I lead a Bible study? And on and on! Nobody has even asked me how I am, how I am adjusting. They never asked what they can do for me. Talk about feeling labeled! My identity is wrapped up in what they think I can do for them. I just want to pull the covers over my head and stay in bed."

That was the first time I realized the kind of struggle so many pastors' wives have in moving, and yet people in their congregations expect them to jump in and start serving them. We need to be sensitive to their needs; they have to adjust just like anyone else.

Dusty and overlooked. She feels like she's been stuffed in the closet or pushed under the bed, totally disregarded. A "dusty mover" told me in a weary voice, "Moving is so traumatic for me that my husband has stopped asking me if I want to move again. He just tells me we *are* moving again. He doesn't even consider my feelings about another move."

Worn-out and wasted. She's just so far gone, she can't be put back together again. When I met a "worn-out mover" in our Moving On class at church, the first thing she said to me was, "I'm so tired from this move. I'm exhausted from unpacking and setting up our home. My husband started traveling immediately. That left me with taking care of our four children and everything else that needed to be done."

Frazzled and frayed. She has had so much piled on top of her that she's crying out, "I can't take anymore! Don't ask me to do one more thing until I get unpacked!" She's totally overwhelmed with an endless to-do list.

Scared and alone. She has been mishandled by life. Divorced and self-supporting with two children, one mover like this had just moved here to get away from the pain of the past. Afraid and alone, she didn't know how to start over again, and she came to our church looking for a place to belong. She found our Moving On group and made new friends who came alongside her in her time of need. "These women showed me unconditional love that I have never known," she said.

Bent and bothered. As I saw her walking toward me, I could tell this mover was bent out of shape. All she did was complain. She complained about living in Arizona; she complained about the heat; she complained about the desert. Nothing pleased her. "Why did the company have to move us here?" she whined in a high voice.

Coming apart at the seams. She's on the verge of losing it. She and her husband had been in Phoenix only six months when he lost his job. Their house payments were already more than they could afford, and if something didn't change quickly, they would lose their home. The stress of it all was beginning to affect their marriage. She said, "I'm falling apart. What will happen to us?"

Shut tight by a broken zipper. She won't open up and she's lost her zip. When she came to our class, she sat by herself. Her smile was forced. She didn't say much, but I knew she was hiding behind the pain of her move. It took weeks for her to finally begin to tell her story. She and her husband had moved ten times in thirteen years of marriage. It had become easier for her to remain detached than to open up to new relationships. She looked into my eyes and said, "It's too painful to have to say good-bye again and again."

When I think of suitcases, I can just envision a family luggage set. It might look something like this:

- 26-inch Pullman—the father
- 24-inch Pullman—the mother
- 21-inch carry-ons—the children
- Hanging bag—the teenagers

Where do you fit? Maybe you feel like a 26-inch Pullman because you've had to be the heavyweight, the one in charge. Maybe you feel like the carry-on because you had no choice about coming here. Maybe you feel like the hanging bag because of your hang-ups about this move. Or could it be you don't even feel like a part of the set—instead you feel like a bag that's never been unpacked from previous moves?

Go for the Designer Luggage

Sometimes, in my weaker moments, I imagine replacing my old mustard-colored vinyl bag—the one with the large, ugly zipper—with new designer luggage. I'd like the kind that is covered with floral-print fabric. Mine would have big cabbage roses in shades of pink and wheels that glide through an airport. It would have lots of zippered compartments to put all my special little things in, and it would be stain and tear resistant. On the sturdy handle would be a fancy little gold lock that only I could open. Wouldn't that be great?

I think designer luggage is constructed by someone who obviously knows a lot about luggage and a lot about people.

Heart to Heart

If I could be with you right this moment, we'd have our heart-to-heart talk and a cup of coffee. This is what I would tell you: Perhaps it's time for you to think about exchanging your old beat-up suitcase for new luggage, designed for you by your Master Designer (in other words, exchange your old life for a new life in Christ). What your Master Designer provides can be an anchor in your life and in all the moves you'll ever make. You will never travel alone again, and the best part is that the Master Designer Himself will accompany you wherever you go.

You'll be identified as a woman who trusts God as her Master Designer. He can handle all your moving situations, no matter what— or where—they are.

With your Master Designer:

> *You are tagged for the right destination.* You know that all the moves during your lifetime are just temporary. Your eternal destination will be permanent.
>
> *You are marked with God's "special handling" label.* God restores the weary. He comforts the worn-out, frazzled, and frayed. He protects the scarred-up. He strengthens those coming apart at the seams. He renews the dusty and bent-in, and He heals the broken.
>
> *You are secure in God's love.* Nothing—absolutely nothing, nor any amount of miles—can separate you from the love of God.
>
> *You are sturdy.* God is holding on to you. He will not let you go!

Scriptures for a Well-Worn Mover

The LORD will continually guide you ... and give strength to your bones; and you will be like a watered garden.

ISAIAH 58:11

So we do not look at what we can see right now, the troubles all around us, but we look forward to the joys in heaven which we have not yet seen. The troubles will soon be over, but the joys to come will last forever.

2 CORINTHIANS 4:18, TLB

The LORD himself watches over you! The LORD stands beside you as your protective shade. The sun will not harm you by day, nor the moon at night. The LORD keeps you from all harm and watches over your life. The LORD keeps watch over you as you come and go, both now and forever.

PSALM 121:5-8, NLT

I have loved you with an everlasting love; therefore I have drawn you with lovingkindness.

JEREMIAH 31:3

Do not fear, for I have redeemed you; I have called you by name; you are Mine! When you pass through the waters, I will be with you; and through the rivers, they will not overflow you. When you walk through the fire, you will not be scorched, nor will the flame burn you.

ISAIAH 43:1-2

For I am convinced that neither death, nor life, nor angels, nor principalities, nor things present, nor things to come, nor powers, nor height, nor depth, nor any other created thing, will be able to separate us from the love of God, which is in Christ Jesus our Lord.

ROMANS 8:38-39

In this chapter, we've had a little fun talking about identifying with our luggage and finding out about some real-life labels we wear. Now that you've looked at the outside, how do you feel on the inside? When I opened the suitcase of my life, I found many feelings about our moves and how they had affected me. I had stuffed a lot of emotions inside until after our last move, when I finally began to deal with them. I would have liked it better if my feelings and emotions had been neatly folded and packed in my suitcase at each move; but so many times I just threw them in, closed the lid on them, and rushed on to the next move. All the while, my load became heavier and heavier.

What emotional baggage are you still dragging behind from your move? Can you identify the luggage tags that describe your feelings and emotions? In the next chapter, we're going to take a look *inside* your suitcase!

CHAPTER 7

REMOVE YOUR LUGGAGE TAGS!

Then David left his baggage in the care of the baggage keeper.
I SAMUEL 17:22

I REMEMBER THE emotional baggage I carried after our move to Phoenix. Even though the physical baggage I brought with me had long since been unpacked and neatly put away, I still had emotional baggage that had never been opened and looked at after our moves. These were emotions and feelings I needed to identify and work through in order to start over and move forward. I struggled with comparison, feelings of inadequacy, and loss of identity. Yes, I even struggled with anger. In fact, you name it, I probably felt it!

Southern sundresses, homes with basements and attics, BIG yards, the word *y'all*, and the beauty of four seasons were suddenly compared with the jeans-and-boots look, no extra storage space, my "dog run" yard, the phrase *you guys*, and one long, hot summer.

In the areas of my life where I once felt confident, I now felt extremely inadequate. I used to be able to zip around town in no time, knowing just where to go for what I needed. Then we moved and I had no idea where I was going; I just hoped I would end up at the right place and be home before dark. I had always been so outgoing and such a "take charge" person. With this move, I became withdrawn and would find myself sitting quietly in the back row at church. I was discouraged with my new life and yearned for a friend who *really* knew me. I was angry with Bill and his company for moving us here. I would sit and cry, cry and sit, and take long naps in the afternoon.

Yet I can say that with time, a change of attitude, and a redirected focus on God, I began to love living here. This is where my home is and my heart belongs. I will be honest; it didn't happen overnight, or over a month.

But through the process, my life became reframed around Jesus Christ—a game changer for me.

Identify Your Own Luggage Tags

In chapter 6, we talked about how some women identify with what their luggage looks like on the outside. In this chapter, we are going to identify luggage tags that label the feelings and emotions we carry inside—much like all the "stuff" we carry inside our suitcases. Now that I've identified some of my feelings and emotions, let's take a closer look at others that might be all too familiar to you.

Here are some luggage tags you might be wearing since your move:

Anger. Are you harboring anger because you didn't want to move?
Bitterness. Do you feel bitter because this move has caused major changes in your life?
Comparison. Do you find yourself comparing everything to where you used to live, and comparing yourself to everyone else?
Fear. Do you fear the unknown: Will you like it here? Will the job work out? Will the children adjust?
Anxiety. Are you anxious about making new friends and finding the right school, church, doctor, grocery store, cleaners, and other places or services you need?

Disappointment. Is the house not what you really wanted? Is the job a disillusionment? Is the cost of living higher?

Loss of identity. Has your self-esteem taken a nose-dive? Have you gotten lost in the shuffle?

Depression. Is everything overwhelming and you'd rather stay in bed than unpack a box, hang a picture, or fix a meal?

Expectations. Were you expecting the neighbors to be friendly? Expecting to find a close friend by now? Expecting everything to fit in your house?

Inadequacy. Do you feel like you just don't have what it takes anymore—personally or professionally?

Hurt. Do the tears come when you think of family, friends, or places you left behind? Perhaps there was a severed relationship and the issue has not been resolved.

Grief. Are you grieving over all your losses?

What emotions do you need to identify and begin to unpack?

She Hates the Weather and the Bugs

Margaret moved away from Virginia and is miserable in Iowa, longing to be back in her former home. She is still wearing so many luggage tags and is still in so much pain from her move that she's leading a life of misery and despair. The fact is, six months after their move she still hasn't adjusted, and it's having a ripple effect on her children and her marriage. She harbors great anger and bitterness toward her husband for moving them to Iowa. Even though they bought a new home and had it beautifully decorated and landscaped, even though they are going to a great church nearby, and even though she has everything that would appear to make her happy, she said to me not long ago, "I hate it here; my life is so empty. There isn't anything about this place I like."

She told me that she hates the weather and that the bugs are terrible. When I asked her children how *they* like living there, they said, "It's always raining, and the bugs are everywhere!" See the ripple effect?

Young children mirror what they see and hear within the home. Then they begin to have those same feelings.

Margaret's marriage is also drifting apart. She resents Sam for being so busy with his new job. "He doesn't seem to have time for me anymore, and we used to be inseparable." They no longer have any quality time alone when Sam isn't working. Any leftover time goes to the children and their activities. It seems Margaret and Sam live in two separate worlds and the distance between them is growing. Margaret is still wearing the luggage tags of anger, bitterness, and resentment that have kept her from starting over and moving forward with her life.

Which emotional luggage tags are you still wearing? What feelings and emotions are keeping you from starting over and going forward after your move? This is the best time to stop and take a good look at those tags—to identify them one by one, acknowledge what they are doing to you and your family, and make the choice to begin to release them.

David Can Show You How

I have often compared the "giant" luggage tags we wear with the Bible story of David and the giant, Goliath. David had to overcome and defeat Goliath, the giant in his life. You have to overcome the giants you face daily: anger, fear, bitterness, discouragement, expectations, comparison, anxiety, inadequacy, disappointment, hurt, frustration, loss of identity, or other issues.

Whatever your giants may be, there is much to learn from David (see 1 Samuel 17).

David left his baggage in the care of the baggage keeper (see v. 22). He left behind the things that would encumber him and keep him from moving forward to get to the battle line to defeat Goliath.

You can leave your baggage in the care of your personal Baggage Keeper—Jesus Christ. He is the one who can carry all your "stuff." Nothing is too heavy for Him. Not only will He lighten your load; He will bear your burdens. He will equip you to face your giants and overcome them.

In other words, lay it down at the feet of Jesus. *Daily* let it go.

REMOVE YOUR LUGGAGE TAGS! || 69

Daily remind yourself that you are not going to fight this battle alone. Yes, I said *daily*. It's so easy to pick your baggage back up, in your own strength, and try to handle or manage life all by yourself. It is an everyday battle, my friends.

I, too, have to choose to leave whatever giant I'm facing for the day at the feet of Jesus. Many a day, He carries me in His arms because I'm too weak to stand alone. I fight the battle of emptiness with the loss of Bill. Many a day, I fight feeling overwhelmed with house maintenance, ministry needs, people needs, and even my own emotional needs. Some days I fight feeling inadequate to write or speak, and I battle the giant of comparison. There are times when unpredictable grief washes over me like waves in the ocean. Emptiness, feeling overwhelmed, inadequacy, comparison, grief—these are all giants that I choose to fight, as I lay them down daily and give them to my Baggage Keeper.

Leaving your baggage with your Baggage Keeper to face the giants in your life is vital as you choose to:

> *Let go,*
> > *Start over, and*
> > > *Move forward with your life.*

You may not know how or where to begin the process, so here are some steps to help you get started. Let's take a look at how we can be like David.

Rely on God's faithfulness (see v. 37). Just as David recalled God's faithfulness to him in the past, recall the times of God's faithfulness in your life. Be specific.

Be yourself. Don't try to be someone you're not! In verses 38-39, David realized that the garments Saul clothed him with weren't right for him, so he took them off and went to face Goliath just as he was—a shepherd boy with five stones and a sling. When you move to a new place, face your new life just as you are, in the beauty of who God made you to be. Don't try to be accepted by trying to be like everyone else.

Be equipped. Take these five smooth stones (see v. 40) to face your giants:

1. *Faith.* Have the kind of faith David had when he reached down in the brook for five stones, knowing that killing the giant was an impossible task without God's help. He recognized his own weakness but had the faith to know he could face Goliath with God's strength.
2. *Prayer.* Don't even attempt to stand up to your giants until you go down on your knees in prayer! You can't fight anger with anger, but you can fight anger with prayer.
3. *Bible study.* The more you know and study God's Word, the firmer the ground you stand on will be! God's Word will keep you on track with His truth and His promises.
4. *Fellowship.* Seek out the fellowship of Christian friends— for support, for accountability, for group Bible study, for encouragement, for fun! Great strength lies in numbers. It's important not to feel alone as we face the obstacles that we need to overcome.
5. *Perseverance.* Don't give up and don't give in. David didn't give up in spite of Goliath's size and strong voice of intimidation and belittling (see vv. 43-44). What voices are you hearing that tell that you can't do it, that you can't overcome your giants?

Here are three more important choices to make to win against the giants:

- *Be not afraid* "for the battle is the LORD's" (v. 47). Your part, like David's, is to be willing, to be prepared, and to be confident in the Lord.
- *Be quick.* "David ran quickly toward the battle line" (v. 48). Don't delay in confronting the giant in your life that's hurting you, your husband, your children, or your relationship with God.

* *Be bold.* "David put his hand into his bag and took from it a stone and slung it" (v. 49). Then he trusted God for the results. Trust God with all your heart, with all your soul, and with all your might for the results. Pick up your stones and take action!

I shared all of this with my friend Margaret the last time I saw her. She cried as she began to recognize the luggage tags that were still attached to her from her move. I just held her, listening as she talked. (Listening is one of the greatest gifts you can give a newcomer. They yearn to speak their thoughts and have someone interested enough to listen.)

"I see what's been happening to me," she said. "I see how I've held on to this anger at Sam for moving us here and how it's built walls between us. For the first time, I'm really seeing how negative the children have become. I've resented the time Sam puts into work, yet I know it's all part of this new promotion."

Slowly, she began to identify the pain in her life. We talked again about "leaving your baggage with the Baggage Keeper" and how you can "give your burdens to the LORD, and he will take care of you" (Psalm 55:22, NLT).

"You can leave all this emotional baggage, all these luggage tags that keep you from starting over and moving forward, all these giants that cast a shadow over your life, at the feet of Jesus," I told Margaret. "Just pick up your stones and take action!" I caught a glimpse of hope in her eyes. I knew this was a turning point in her life. I suggested she and Sam make time to go out to dinner, go for a walk, go on a picnic—anything, as long as she could talk to him and start sharing her feelings. It was clear that Margaret had not told Sam how she was feeling, and the longer she kept her emotions inside, the more hardened she became.

Margaret then did a rather clever thing. She met Sam on his own turf. She made a lunch appointment with him and began a once-a-week-set-aside-time-for-me opportunity to talk. With this one-on-one time, away from home and office, Sam began to understand the changes that had taken place in his wife since they had moved. Now he understood why he had been feeling so rejected. The rejection had caused him to work harder and longer. The lunches have since become evenings out, and the walls are coming down between them. Margaret is seeking the positive rather than the negative in their new city. She's beginning to discover the uniqueness that Iowa has to offer.

She and the children are making a scrapbook of "Things to Do and Places to Go" for the children's grandparents in Virginia.

"Don't just go to church, Margaret," I told her. "Get *involved* in church. Join a women's Bible study or a couples' group, or volunteer to serve in some way." I knew that in a small-group setting she would begin to make friends and form relationships. Margaret called me a few months later to say that, with time, a change of attitude, and a redirected focus on God, her life is changing and she is moving beyond her pain.

"Yes," I said, smiling as my eyes filled with tears of joy, "I understand exactly what you mean!" Many of you face the same circumstances as Margaret and can relate as well.

Each time you move, you acquire a new kind of luggage tag. The important thing is not to allow those labels to misdirect you and keep sending you back into a moving meltdown. You will face giants daily, whether you move or not. It's critical to recognize and acknowledge what the "giant" luggage tags are, come face-to-face with them, and then:

- Leave your emotional baggage with your Baggage Keeper.
- Rely on God's faithfulness.
- Be who you are.
- Be equipped.
- Don't be afraid.
- Be quick.
- Be bold.
- Trust God for the results!

I wanted Margaret to release and replace the luggage tags of feelings and emotions that could easily become giants in her life. I suggested that she copy this list and keep it handy for reference. You might want to do the same thing.

Replace Your Luggage Tags

Anger or bitterness with forgiveness

Get rid of all bitterness, rage, anger, harsh words, and slander, as well as all types of evil behavior. Instead, be kind to each other, tenderhearted, forgiving one another, just as God through Christ has forgiven you.

EPHESIANS 4:31-32, NLT

Don't let the sun go down with you still angry.

EPHESIANS 4:26, TLB

Comparison with contentment

A relaxed attitude lengthens a man's life; jealousy rots it away.

PROVERBS 14:30, TLB

I have learned to be content in whatever circumstances I am.

PHILIPPIANS 4:11

Fear with courage

Don't be afraid, for I am with you. Don't be discouraged, for I am your God. I will strengthen you and help you.

ISAIAH 41:10, NLT

When I am afraid, I will put my trust in You.

PSALM 56:3

Anxiety with assurance

Don't worry about things—food, drink, and clothes. For you already have life and a body—and they are far more important than what to eat and wear. Look at the birds! They don't worry about what to eat—they don't need to sow or reap

or store up food—for your heavenly Father feeds them. And you are far more valuable to him than they are.
MATTHEW 6:25-26, TLB

Give all your worries to Him because He cares for you.
I PETER 5:7, NLV

Disappointment with fulfillment

Now glory be to God, who by his mighty power at work within us is able to do far more than we would ever dare to ask or even dream of.
EPHESIANS 3:20, TLB

The Lord will work out his plans for my life.
PSALM 138:8, TLB

Loss of identity with security

I have called you by name; you are mine. . . . You are precious to me and honored, and I love you.
ISAIAH 43:1,4, TLB

If I take the wings of the dawn, if I dwell in the remotest part of the sea, even there Your hand will lead me, and Your right hand will lay hold of me.
PSALM 139:9-10

Depression with hope

Now may the God of hope fill you with all joy and peace.
ROMANS 15:13

My hope is from Him. He only is my rock and my salvation, my stronghold; I shall not be shaken.
PSALM 62:5-6

Read the entire book of Psalms!

Discouragement with encouragement

By not giving up, God's Word gives us strength
and hope.

ROMANS 15:4, NLV

I was given strength, because the hand of the Lord
my God was upon me.

EZRA 7:28, NLV

Expectations with gratitude

Set your mind on the things above, not on the things
that are on earth.

COLOSSIANS 3:2

Whatever is good and perfect comes to us from God.

JAMES 1:17, NLV

Inadequacy with confidence

For the LORD will be your confidence.

PROVERBS 3:26

Such confidence we have through Christ toward God.
Not that we are adequate in ourselves to consider
anything as coming from ourselves, but our adequacy
is from God.

2 CORINTHIANS 3:4-5

Hurt with healing

He heals the brokenhearted and binds up their wounds.

PSALM 147:3

For I, the LORD, am your healer.

EXODUS 15:26

Grief with comfort

> We give thanks to the God and Father of our Lord Jesus
> Christ. He is our Father Who shows us loving-kindness and
> our God Who gives us comfort. He gives us comfort in all
> our troubles. Then we can comfort other people who have
> the same troubles. We give the same kind of comfort God
> gives us.
>
> 2 CORINTHIANS 1:3-4, NLV

> My soul weeps because of grief; strengthen me according to
> Your word.
>
> PSALM 119:28

 ## Heart to Heart

My dear new friends, the one thing to remember from this day forward, now and always, is this: The only luggage tag you will want to
wear, and will want to claim as your own, is the one that says, "I am a
child of God! I am a daughter of the King!"

Now that we've come this far together, I hope you'll also consider
me as someone who understands and cares about you. Continue to let
go and allow God to mend you. Hold this verse in your heart: "I can
do all things through Him who strengthens me" (Philippians 4:13).

I'm excited about getting into the next section in which we begin
the journey of Starting Over. Where do we begin? Within ourselves,
within our homes, and within our families.

PART 2

Start Over

In part 1, we walked together through the process of letting go. My prayer is that you are now equipped with a deeper understanding that the choice to let go affects your ability to start over and move forward. If you are still working through letting go, that's okay. No one will be at the same place, at the same time, on this journey. The important thing is that you don't get stuck along the way. I only ask that you will choose daily to be open to God's leading as He guides you on the path to letting go. When you begin to focus on the present, and not the past, you'll be ready to start over.

Here are some of the things we will be unpacking in the following chapters:

Create your home.
Bloom where you are.
Keep your marriage strong, not stressed.
Help your children with the transition.
Accept a degree of loneliness.
Discover your identity.
Make new friends.
Reach out to your neighbors.

This is where we're going to get up close and personal, my friends. Remember, as you start over, God will mold a new you!

CHAPTER 8

CREATE A NEW NEST

Anybody can build a house; we need the Lord for the
creation of a home.

JOHN HENRY JOWETT

ONCE THE BOXES WERE UNPACKED, I would begin creating a place for our family to nest and call home.

As part of that process, the first thing our family did when we moved into a house was to hang our hammock in the yard. The last thing we did before moving out was to take it down.

For as long as I can remember, a hammock has been a part of my life and a tradition in our home for generations. As a child, part of the anticipation of going to my grandmother's house included running up the steps to the big front porch and jumping into the hammock where I could swing to my heart's content. Mama and Daddy gave one to us when we got married and we continued to pass the hammock tradition on to the next generation. The hammock has become a symbol of home to our family.

The kind of hammock I still have is a large crisscross, white cotton rope swing that hooks to two large trees. Two people can lie in the hammock at the same time; more can sit in it and swing as long as they like. Now that you can picture my hammock, let's pretend that we are swinging in it together. We can visit, and I will share with you the things you need to know as you create your *new* nest.

The Nest Builders

One day I noticed part of the rope on my hammock was loose and hanging down. Since this had never happened before, I took a closer look. Obviously, the rope had frayed at the end, causing it to weaken and come loose. *How could this have happened?* I wondered. And so I watched closely throughout the day. Much to my amazement, I saw two little birds fly down and tug at the rope end until they pulled a piece loose. They flew off with the fragments in their mouths to a thick honeysuckle vine growing up the wall of our house. I quietly peeked through the vine to discover a nest made of *my hammock rope!* The birds had created a nest of rope mixed with grass and twigs. Being the bird lover that I am (one of my missions in life is to feed every bird that regularly stops in my yard), I didn't disturb the nest. I just moved the hammock from its prime location to another spot.

As I watched the mama bird and her babies in their nest, I was reminded of similar ways we can "nest" in our new homes. We have to start with quality nest-building essentials to give our homes firm foundations.

There are four things I want to pass on to you about the nest-building process.

1. *First, and most important, is to weave your nest with the fruit of the Spirit:* love, joy, peace, patience, kindness, goodness, faithfulness, gentleness, and self-control (see Galatians 5:22-23).

   All these qualities will become part of the fiber of your nest, as a result of knowing and loving Jesus Christ. They are the inner qualities that you practice, not preach, in your home. It is all about *who* you are, rather than *what* you can do. God will work in you to bring about a Christlikeness in your life, and that Christlikeness will ultimately be reflected in your home.

A friend once told me after we had talked about nest-building, "I'm so glad God gives us second chances when we move. I needed to weave more peace and patience into our home. I let my circumstances control me instead of letting God control me. The last time we moved, we were hurting financially and I took my frustration out on the children. Our circumstances haven't changed, but my attitude has. I want to do it differently this time."

She realized her own inadequacies and the difference it would make in her actions and in her home if she let God control her life.

As a woman, you have an enormous amount of influence in your home. You are the pivotal point. You are the catalyst for what happens there. A dear friend always says, "If Mama ain't happy, ain't nobody happy!" How true it is! As you weave the essence of who you are into your nest, your attitudes and actions will spill over to affect your husband and children.

If you are frazzled, your home will appear frazzled. If you are peaceful, your home will reflect your peace. If you are happy, your family will "catch it," because happiness is contagious. If you yell at your family, that too can be contagious.

The strongest nest-building quality available to you is Christ in you. He will weave Himself in and through you, that you might reflect Him through the fruit of the Spirit.

2. *It doesn't matter what kind of nest you have; the important thing is, wherever you are, make it a home—a sanctuary.* Some birds live in fancy birdhouses and others in nests of twigs. Your nest may be a house, an apartment, a patio home, a condo, or a mobile home. Women will say to me, "But I don't have a house; I live in an apartment. Why should I even try to nest in?" Wrong! The place you live is an extension of yourself, the essence of who you are. It reveals your identity. Christ can be revealed anywhere you live. He's not picky.

Take Stephanie, for example. She and her husband live with their baby in a small mobile home. Their home is truly a place of loveliness. Pots of flowers on the porch greet visitors. The eat-in kitchen has a bay window with colorful curtains. On the table are fresh flowers. Stephanie has decorated each room economically and attractively and made it a warm and inviting haven. Her home reveals who she is and expresses what she believes, and who she believes in. My friend loves being a wife and mother, and she has learned to be content in her circumstances. Stephanie and her home reflect the peace and joy that come from her strong relationship with God. It is obvious that the presence of Christ lives in their home, and that love and faith are woven into their nest for a firm foundation.

Another friend, Susie, is a baby boomer. She's retired and finds she doesn't need as large a home as she did when she was raising a family. She and her husband are ready to live a simpler, clutter-free life, with less stuff. Their nest will look different as they downsize to a smaller home, a condo, a patio home, or an apartment. Because of health issues, some boomers or their parents will have to move into assisted-living facilities and relinquish everything but a few mementos.

As the years go by for me, I have learned how little I really need to be happy and comfortable. It's not *things* that make me happy, though I used to think it was. No matter where I might live, I'll spread a little sunshine in each room with whatever I have. When someone walks in my door I can embrace them with the love of Jesus, a glass of tea, and warm friendship. Nesting can be as simple as that, my friends, no matter where we live.

3. *Even if you are in your nest for only a few weeks, months, or just a year before moving on, make an effort to settle in and create a home for your family.*
   You will never regret the effort you made. Take a lesson from

the birds. Like us, some birds don't stay in one place very long; they vacate their nests and move on. Yet no matter how long a bird occupies a nest, she makes it a home for her family. It is her number one priority.

In our mobile society there are many temporary, short-term assignments. Large companies, the civil service, the military, and missions agencies, just to name a few, routinely move families every one to three years. Unless we make nest-building a priority, it can easily get lost in the short-term shuffle.

When Bill was in the Air Force, we lived in a one-bedroom efficiency apartment for less than a year. It would have been so easy to leave our pictures and accessories in boxes. After all, we weren't going to be there for long, so what difference would it make? The difference was that Bill and I needed a place to belong, regardless of how short our stay might be. I decided that wherever we were living, I would always make a home for us.

First, I needed to make sure the particular nest-building qualities of love, joy, and peace in our home were my focus. Then, to add my personal touch, I'd put out the welcome mat, set a plant by the front door, and arrange either inexpensive flowers from the grocery store or fresh greenery from the yard on the kitchen table. Then I'd hang pictures and place some of our favorite accessories around the house. That way, no matter where we lived, when Bill walked in the front door, he would feel he had come home.

After the children arrived, I needed to focus on the nest-building qualities of patience, goodness, and gentleness! I continued to add the personal touches of home when we moved. It was important that our children felt the warmth of familiarity around them. It speeded up their process of putting down roots.

My dear moving friends, don't ever think *temporary*. The imprint of a home today will make a lasting impression for tomorrow in the lives of your family.

4. *The last observation I made about those little birds outside my house was how much order there was in their nest.* It was obvious the nest was there to provide shelter, security, food, and a safe place to grow. All the young birds lined up with their tiny mouths open, waiting to be fed. They depended on their mother to take care of them.

No matter how disorganized and temporary you may feel, your family looks to you to provide their safety, security, encouragement, nurturing love, and daily physical needs.

A single missionary living in Guam says it well. "I have a Bible study and disciple young women from broken homes in my apartment every week. I may not have many material things, but I can provide what these young people don't have in their own homes—a safe environment, a hot meal, acceptance, and unconditional love."

What is the condition of your nest? Is it order or confusion? Remember, "God is not a God of confusion" (1 Corinthians 14:33). Your home will be ordered by God if you put your trust in Him, place your security in Him, depend on Him to meet your needs, and base your values on His Word. It all goes back to being Christ-centered in your life and in your home. When you are, you will then be equipped to feed your family with biblical truths and provide the tools they need for growth.

You Are Not Forgotten

I'm sensitive to the different circumstances many of you face when you move. My heart is heavy when I realize that an overwhelming number of you are *single moms* who have carried all the responsibilities for your home, even when moving. Moving is a physical and emotional strain on *anyone*, let alone someone who is trying to do it solo. You've probably thought at one time or another, *I'm a single mom. I don't have the time to create a nest.* Oh, but you do, and you have the very best reason of all—your children. Your children need to experience, on a daily basis, the nest-building qualities of the fruit of the Spirit reflected in you.

They need to see that your life is centered on Christ and not your circumstances. God will strengthen you. Never give up; never lose heart.

If you are *single without children*, let me remind you that you, too, are not alone. Christ can fill your home and your heart with a peace and a fullness that comes only from a relationship with Him. When you are settling in, create a nest that you love to come home to at the end of the day, one that brings you comfort and a place to belong. Create a place to welcome new friends.

You might be *divorced* or *widowed*, downsizing to a smaller home and feeling too overwhelmed to create anything, much less another home. Even though you are starting over, you still have Jesus, who will fill the empty rooms of your heart with His presence. Let His nest-building qualities flow from within you as you create a new nest.

Perhaps *retirement* is the reason you've moved, and it's a new beginning at this season of your life. As you re-create your nest with all the essentials of what you need, don't ever forget how much you still need Jesus. He doesn't ever retire!

Some of you may feel as if you're moving alone because your husband doesn't share your faith. *Even if only one person in a family knows Jesus Christ, reflects His love, and weaves a nest with Christlike qualities, it will have a positive impact on the unbelievers in the family.*

If you are that one person, your part is to keep believing and keep weaving.

Weave the Fruit of the Spirit into Your Nest

Unpacking the boxes, getting the rooms set up, adding accessories, and hanging the pictures are all essential for creating a nest to call home. It doesn't matter if you have the most beautifully decorated and organized home in the world, however—if you don't *live out* the fruit of the Spirit daily to your family and friends, nothing else really matters. Will you live out all of the fruit, all the time? Of course not. You'll have times when you lose your patience, don't feel joyful, or aren't loving. The important thing to remember is that the fruit of God's Spirit lives within you. It is your choice to share it with others.

Love

> [Love] bears all things, believes all things, hopes all things,
> endures all things.
>
> I CORINTHIANS 13:7

Love is the centering point from which to weave your new nest. Love weathers the storms in life with faith and endurance for today and hope for tomorrow. Some practical ways you can express your love are often found in the little things, such as:

A smile
A hug
A touch
A word of encouragement
A word of praise
A word of affirmation
A love note that reads, "I'm so glad we're all here together as we
    start over."
An act of kindness
A listening ear

For a time after you move, your family may be a little fragile and may need an extra measure of tender, loving care. Let love permeate your home like the fragrance of perfume.

How can you demonstrate an observable love to your husband, children, or friends?

Joy

> I have told you these things so My joy may be in you and
> your joy may be full.
>
> JOHN 15:11, NLV

Joy is an attitude and a choice we make. We shouldn't let our joy depend on circumstances; rather, we can have joy in spite of our circumstances.

A moving friend said, "This wasn't the house I wanted. We don't have a yard and there isn't any money left to buy curtains." She said it without whining or acting upset. She continued, "I knew, however, my attitude about what I didn't have would affect my whole family, so I just decided to make the best of the situation. I focused on the positives about the house, put my plants in pots, and got some colorful fabric to make curtains!"

In which circumstances do you need to choose joy?

Peace

You will experience God's peace, which is far more wonderful than the human mind can understand. His peace will keep your thoughts and your hearts quiet and at rest as you trust in Christ Jesus.

PHILIPPIANS 4:7, TLB

Fear will rob you of peace, and a lack of peace will bring anxiety and worry. God's peace will protect your heart, mind, emotions, and thoughts. Without inner tranquility, you can't weave a calm spirit into your new home.

Chris confessed to me, "I'm so afraid to stay in this house alone when my husband travels. If something happened, who would I call in the middle of the night? We don't know anyone yet and the nearest neighbor is a mile away."

That's the kind of worry that creates fear, brings anxiety, and robs you of peace.

What situations in your life need the peace of Christ?

Patience

We can rejoice, too, when we run into problems and trials, for we know that they are good for us—they help us learn to be patient. And patience develops strength of character in us and helps us trust God more each time we use it until finally our hope and faith are strong and steady.

ROMANS 5:3-4, TLB

God taught me more about patience when He had me in a holding pattern than at any other time in my life. The holding pattern occurred when we were waiting for our house in Atlanta to sell. We were in Phoenix eighteen months before it sold. We were strapped with two house payments, and there was nothing we could do but be patient and wait.

Some of you are in a holding pattern as well, and all you can do is wait. Patience allows God to use the circumstances of your move to fulfill His plan for you and develop His character in you. It's enduring without complaining.

I must say that creating a nest with patience was not easy for me then, but in the end I learned to trust God all the more.

When was the last time your patience was tested?

Kindness

Be kind to one another, tender-hearted, forgiving each other, just as God in Christ also has forgiven you.
EPHESIANS 4:32

Kindness begins in your home and then spills over beyond it. I'll never forget the time I was busy making cookies for our Newcomers' Coffee. Ginger, my daughter, came into the kitchen just in time to see me put them on a tray. "Great, Mom! You made cookies for us!" she said as she reached for one. Oops! Guess you know how I felt as I told her they were for church. Guess you know the message that was conveyed to her—that my kindness went to others first, and second to my family. Wrap your own nest in kindness before you spill it over to everyone else.

What act of kindness can you show in your home today?

Goodness

Surely goodness and lovingkindness will follow me all the days of my life, and I will dwell in the house of the LORD forever.
PSALM 23:6

There is a saying that goes, "What you *do* speaks so loudly that I can't hear what you *say*!" The way we live our lives is the best example of goodness. Goodness characterizes a person of moral value, honesty, integrity, virtue, honor, and generosity. What you do and how you live inside your home speaks volumes to your family. They see the real you behind closed doors, and your life is their greatest teacher.

What is one way you can live out goodness?

Faithfulness

We know these things are true by believing, not by seeing.

2 CORINTHIANS 5:7, TLB

To me, faith is an unwavering confidence in God's Word and in His promises. Faith is believing, trusting, and knowing without seeing. You weave your nest every day by faith. I have a small poster on the mirror in my bathroom that says, "Faith isn't faith until it's all you've got left." Sometimes faith is all I have left when I can't *see* the changes or results I've hoped and prayed for. My faith has gotten me through many a tough time when I couldn't see the light at the end of the tunnel.

How have you walked by faith this week?

Gentleness

You should clothe yourselves instead with the beauty that comes from within, the unfading beauty of a gentle and quiet spirit, which is so precious to God.

1 PETER 3:4, NLT

Gentleness is shown in how we treat others. It is love refined through our actions. Weave your nest carefully with thoughtfulness, consideration, respect, and courtesy.

A friend shared, "When I moved into the neighborhood, my neighbor was so considerate to stop by and offer her help. She had moved six months before and was sensitive to my needs. I'll always remember how gentle she was with my fragile emotions."

What are some ways you can show a gentle spirit?

Self-Control

> A gentle answer turns away anger, but a sharp word
> causes anger.
> PROVERBS 15:1, NLV

It doesn't take long for outbursts of anger, quick judgments, and bad attitudes to overshadow all the positive things you've created in your nest. I can't tell you the number of times I've blown it by over-reacting. Where was everybody when I needed help unpacking the boxes? Boy, did I let them have it. Why wasn't Bill home in time for dinner? Was his new job that important? Well, I sure told him! What did I care if the house was never unpacked and the rooms were a mess? See if it bothered me! (I could certainly become the Wicked Witch of the West when I lost my temper.)

How do you struggle to maintain self-control?

As you begin to create a new home, think about the nest-building qualities you might want to focus on or weave into the foundation of your home.

Over the years, I have always given friends who are moving, or newcomers to my area, a little bird's nest with tiny colored eggs in it. It serves as a reminder for them to weave their nest with the fruit of the Spirit. After years of giving these nests, it's heartwarming when I visit a friend's home to see one sitting on a windowsill or kitchen counter and know she has created a "fruitful" nest.

 Heart to Heart

A great word picture for you to remember when creating your home comes from Sylvia Fair's book for children, *The Bedspread.* She tells the wonderful story of two old sisters, Maud and Amelia, who decide to decorate their long, white bedspread by embroidering it. Each works from an end as they create pictures of the house they lived in as children.

As they start to embroider, Maud says, "And we'll begin at the front door." Then Amelia says with a smile, "A very good place to start, dear."

As the design begins to take shape, Maud realizes she's left something out of her intricate stitching. She says to Amelia, "Your house is happy. I forgot to add the happiness."[1]

So always remember, the best place to begin creating a home with the fruit of the Spirit starts at the front door—and don't forget to add the happiness. (And I know where you can get a great swing in a hammock too!)

 ## Unpack Your Survival Box

Twenty-one practical ways to help create your nest and to make your house a home:

1. Put a welcome mat at the front door.
2. Start a tradition with something that symbolizes home to you and your family. When you move, put it out first; when you leave, take it down last—like my hammock.
3. The first time you go to the grocery store, buy a flowering plant or fresh flowers for the kitchen.
4. Make a list of "wanna-do's" for each room. Keep the list with you or in your phone. It's easy to forget what you wanted or needed when you are out shopping.
5. Remember, when you are decorating, less is more.
6. Keep a handy folder or set of folders for information or a card file for business cards to keep as resources. When someone recommends a service (florist, hairdresser, cleaners), jot the information down to save or drop a business card in your file. You can also keep a resource list under Notes in your cell phone or tablet.
7. Go for a new look. Don't be a creature of habit. Just because you did it that way before doesn't mean you have to do it that way this time. Arrange the furniture differently.
8. Rearrange your accessories. Add a new accent color with decorative pillows or a rug.
9. When you meet your neighbors, write down their names and house numbers or save them in your phone, so you won't

forget who lives where. Call them by name the next time you see them.

10. Keep measurements, fabric swatches, paint chips, and wallpaper samples in an envelope in the car. Be prepared for a decorating sale.

11. Remember that a room looks more interesting if you mix different kinds of furniture and accessories instead of having everything match.

12. Don't overdo your decorating. You can always add something later.

13. Don't try too hard to impress with expensive furniture and accessories just because you're new in town. Shop at flea markets, thrift shops, and antique malls for the best buys.

14. Group table accessories and other things in threes or fives.

15. Don't overlook the multitasking basket. It is wonderful for magazines, books, plants, fruit, towels, pictures, cards, or great show-off stuff.

16. Use a scented candle in the kitchen or the bathroom.

17. Start a collection of anything you love. Check out websites to get ideas on displaying your collectibles. They can become great conversation starters when someone comes to your home.

18. Create a home that's comfortable and inviting—not a "show-and-tell" home, but a "touch-and-feel" home.

19. Buy different sizes and shapes of frames to display your pictures. Put them in every room. You can never have too many pictures of smiling faces.

20. Put a wreath on the front door and a smile on your face.

21. *Finally, don't forget to add the happiness!*

Let's turn from the birds and their nests to learn how you can bloom where you're planted!

CHAPTER 9

BLOOM WHERE YOU ARE!

Many of us refuse to grow where we are put, consequently we take root nowhere.

OSWALD CHAMBERS

HAVE YOU EVER PLANTED flowers in your yard and moved before you got to see them bloom? I have. One year I planted flowers in Georgia, and by the time they bloomed the next year, I was planting flowers in North Carolina. I learned from that experience to plant only annuals!

As much as I love birds for the nesting they represent, I love flowers because they help remind me to put down roots wherever I live. I could live in a tent on the beach, but as long as I can somehow plant a flower, I'll be happy. I have had a big yard, a little yard, and even no yard. But I've always had flowers growing, either in the ground or in pots.

Presently, I have the typical Arizona yard in the front—*rocks!* But you should see my little evergreen (read "artificial") grass backyard. Our backyard is so small that Bill always said we should "plant" artificial grass. He would be pleased to know I finally did just that. My patio looks so pretty, even if I do say so myself. I spent twenty-five dollars on colorful bedding plants, planted them in clay pots, and arranged them

93

in groups of three. They provide me with cut flowers for the kitchen and remind me that my roots grow here.

But that's not all. Outside my window I have two bird feeders that draw a crowd of supporters, even as I write. The flowers in my hanging basket and the birds who feed outside are like dear friends who cheer me along through each chapter.

I know that moving can be a confusing, overwhelming time. If I could reach out and touch you right now, I'd give you a big, comforting hug. I know how deeply you long to feel rooted and secure. Consider me your cheerleader on the sidelines, encouraging you along with each new chapter in your life. Now, let's begin to break new ground together!

Breaking New Ground

I love asparagus ferns. They require little care and will grow in either sun or shade. The only thing you have to remember is that they easily become root-bound. The roots crowd until there is no room for growth. They can even take over the soil. When this happens to my ferns, I have to take the plant out of the pot, put it in a larger one, and add fresh soil and fertilizer. You always know that repotting is successful when the fern gets greener and new growth appears.

A moving friend, Alice, is married to an airline pilot. They had lived comfortably in Dallas for eight years. Their root system was heavily intertwined with family, friends, and church. But during an airline cutback, he lost his job. Alice was devastated. She knew they would be forced to move in order for her husband to get another job.

Their move brought them to Phoenix. A year later she said to me, "I thought my world had come to an end. I didn't want to leave Dallas. We were so happy and comfortable there. When we came to Phoenix, I was miserable for about six months. Then we got involved in a great church that made an impact on our lives through the teaching of God's Word. We've made wonderful friends through our church and we even host a small-group Bible study in our home. My husband makes more money at his new job, flies less, and is home with us more than he used to be. I even have a chance to fulfill my dream of going back to college. This move has turned into a blessing in our lives!"

Their move was a forced transplant, much like the move of the fern to a bigger pot. But because Alice and her husband were forced out of their comfort zones, they were put into a situation that gave them more room to grow. Their new roots were enriched by the teaching they received from God's Word, the Christian friends they met, and their new lifestyle. It was obvious to Alice, when she looked back over the life changes they made during that first year, that they had been transplanted by God's hand. She had experienced the normal shock of adjustment but then realized how all the seeds for new growth had come as a result of being uprooted and breaking new ground.

Breaking Ground Alone

Those of you who break new ground alone are among the growing number of single movers who uproot and seek new soil. The *single woman* moving for a job opportunity or to further her education may welcome her transplant as a new challenge and a new experience. The *single parent* may be looking for a fresh start and a way to distance herself from old memories and surroundings. In either case, moving can be twice as hard and stressful when you are alone.

The question many single women ask is not, "Why am I moving?" but rather, "How am I going to move by myself?" Transplanting is much harder without additional hands to help till the soil. To get help loading and unloading your belongings, consider contacting a high school or nearby college to ask if they have a program for students working community-service hours for school credit. Perhaps a church has a volunteer support group that can lend a hand also.

A single mover is just as eager as anyone to put down roots and bloom where she's planted. What does she go through when she moves? The feelings and emotions are the same whether a woman is single or married; only the circumstances are different.

Sarah has moved four times by herself. "Coming home to an empty house every night is the hardest thing for me," she said. "And when you're new to a group, it's very frightening to walk into a room of strangers by yourself." Sarah suggests three things that helped her when she moved: "Reach out to other single women who may feel the same way you do; find a church and get involved in a small group; and look for community programs that offer activities you are interested in."

At age twenty-two, Julie left her family and friends in Wisconsin to teach school in Arkansas. "The hardest thing for me was that I had no history here. No one knew me. The best thing was that it gave me the opportunity to live life on my own. I wasn't responsible for anyone else." Julie continued, "The first thing I did was to look for a singles' interest group to get involved in. I also realized people weren't necessarily going to come up to me, so I sought out other new teachers like myself." Then she said very firmly, "The important thing is, *don't give up!*"

After her divorce, Marty had to go to work full-time. She needed to simplify her life, so she sold her house and moved. It was difficult to break old ties and leave old friends. Even though she felt it was essential to move, Marty said wisely, "If you can afford to stay where you are, don't make any changes when children are involved. They are already going through enough transition."

Leslie is on staff with Cru and trains missionaries to go all over the world. She has moved six times and faced a cross-cultural adjustment when she moved to the Philippines. "Because I'm on the move, I've always rented a place to live," she said. "The hardest thing for me is that I'm never able to accumulate furniture or possessions. Somehow it's just not practical for me to drag those things around from place to place. Moving has taught me to keep my possessions simple, to learn how to adapt, and to have a less complicated life!"

Leslie believes that attitude and choice make a difference when she moves. She has an attitude of hope, knowing God's plan for her move is good. She chooses to bloom where she's planted.

Leslie continued to share some wonderful advice and insight: "As a single woman, I have a need to be around families, so I adopt a family! It's fun to be included and be a part of their lives for special occasions. When I'm lonely, I try to get beyond myself by reaching out to others in need. I've learned that people are willing to help if you just ask. Don't be afraid to ask for help at your job and at your church. We can't wait for it to happen; we have to make a place for ourselves."

God worked in the lives of these women whether their moves were planned or unexpected, welcome or unwanted. New growth has come to each one of them in the course of being uprooted and persevering to break new ground alone.

Often, God initiates a move to take you out of your comfort zone and enable you to grow in your relationship with Him. Are you starting to see the growth possibilities of your new life in your new surroundings?

How Does Your Garden Grow?

Are you watering your woes or fertilizing your faith? It's easy to water your woes when:

- You can't see the big picture.
- You can't see instant results.
- You can't see the sun shining.
- You don't have the right tools.

Believe me, I have watered my woes many times! When we moved to Phoenix, I couldn't even begin to *see the big picture* of what God was going to do in my life. I couldn't foresee the depth to which He was going to nurture my growth and cause me to bloom! So I started watering my woes.

I wanted *instant results*, and when our house in Atlanta didn't sell, my woes reached flood level. Making two house payments was draining us financially.

Even though it's sunny in Phoenix almost all year long, I couldn't *feel the sun shining* in my life for months after we moved. My transplant was very difficult for me, and emotionally, I was in deep root shock for about a year. In despair, I continued watering my woes.

In God's timing, He supplied just *the right tools* for me to take care of my garden. He gave me a wonderful church home, a nurturing Bible study, and a fellowship of Christian women who came alongside me during the replanting time. My faith became fertilized.

I began to see the big picture and understand that our move was God's plan to bring us closer to Him. During the eighteen months that we made two house payments, God was teaching us to trust Him and to depend on Him completely. Somehow, every month, God provided and the money stretched.

As I saw God's faithfulness in our lives, I started to feel the warmth of the sun and began to adjust to being transplanted. My attitude became more positive and my heart more thankful.

If I made the transition from oak trees to cacti, if I learned to "grow" green grass in the desert, you can do what seems impossible too! No matter where you're transplanted, "let us press on to know [the Lord], and he will respond to us as surely as the coming of dawn or the rain of early spring" (Hosea 6:3, TLB).

Growing Deeper Roots

What is the purpose of garden soil? It surrounds the plant and provides support. It nourishes the roots and provides the needed food for growth. Much like soil is life-giving to a plant, God is life-giving to us. He surrounds us with His love, provides support through His people, nourishes us through His Word, and, in Him, our roots can grow deep. Like a plant, we, too, have the capability to bloom.

Now is the time to think about the kind of soil you want for your life as you're putting down roots. When you move, you have the opportunity to start over and make different choices, so I want to share some insights that may help you.

Remember the parable of the seeds in Matthew 13:3-9? Some seeds were sown on rocky places where the soil had no depth, and because the seeds had no roots, they withered away. The seeds that fell on thorns were choked out. But the seeds that fell on the good soil became fruitful.

You can choose the soil in which you want to be planted. Choose carefully! There are many ways to meet people and make friends. For example, tennis, golf, social clubs, or volunteer work are all worthy social outlets. Some women, however, choose to be involved in any social scene to ease the pain of loneliness that comes with moving. It's easy to slip into the busyness of distraction to escape from loneliness and lose yourself in a life that appears to be fertile and productive. Be aware that making unhealthy choices in what you do, or how you spend your time, could be like placing yourself in shallow soil that has no room for deep roots. The seed withered away and could not grow. Choose your soil wisely. Just because something will produce a flower doesn't mean it's right for your garden.

In order for our roots to grow deeply, we need to be grounded in a life that surrounds us with the nurturing and loving soil that God provides. Then all the other things in our lives can grow and flourish.

The best way to grow healthy plants is to water them regularly without drenching them, to provide ample light and fertilizer as needed, and to prune the branches when necessary. Here are some ways for you to grow deep roots in the soil of God's love.

Water regularly by staying in God's Word. My potted plants are watered daily because they're not in the ground where the sprinkler can reach them. They are separated from the other plants and can dry out easily. Since your move, you may have become separated from God's Word for any number of reasons. Don't dry out! Spend time daily reading the Bible to replenish and restore your soul.

Provide plenty of light by knowing God's truth. As you read His Word, memorize Scripture passages, and believe in His promises, truth will be revealed to you. Tremendous growth will come from allowing God to shine on your life.

Fertilize as needed by being in Christian fellowship. God puts Christ-centered people in your life to nurture you, serve as role models and mentors for you, encourage you, pray for you, and hold you accountable. *Seek out a church home if you haven't already.* Find out if the church has a Moving On After Moving In group to help you through your adjustment.

Prune the branches when necessary. Cutting away all the old branches and dead flowers on a plant encourages new growth. I love to pick withering flowers because the more of them you pinch off, the more the plant will bloom. The more branches you prune, the fuller and greener the bush will become. Likewise, careful pruning allows new growth in your life. Perhaps it's a bad habit or an attitude that needs cutting back. The more you trim, the more Christlike you can become.

Gail MacDonald says it best in her book *High Call, High Privilege.*

Removing the spent blossoms on petunias is essential to new blossoms. Today as I removed the old, I was reminded of how essential it is to my life to enjoy each blossom in my life, but to remember to pull it off when spent and move on to new experiences. Many live trying to keep memories of dead blossoms alive only to miss the potential of the new and present bloom.[1]

May your roots go down deep into the soil of God's marvelous love.

EPHESIANS 3:17, TLB

Weary or Worn Out?

Sometimes, regardless of doing the right things, you might still find yourself worn-out and weary from the physical and emotional toll of moving. "How can I bloom," you ask, "when I'm simply exhausted and overwhelmed?"

I get it. I've been there—so weary, so worn-out, that I would fall in bed every night knowing there was still so much to do, and that my list would be there to greet me the next morning. I really think I was borderline burned-out—all from the stress of moving and getting settled in a new place and a new life.

As one young woman said in a prayer request to our ministry, "This is the most stressful move I could imagine. My husband works long hours and travels more in his job. I am pregnant; our house is a fixer-upper and a *mess*; we have no family or friends close by; I homeschool our five-year-old, and, quite frankly, I am an emotional wreck." Her life is not only overwhelming; she is at a breaking point.

In response to my new moving friend, I provided a few practical suggestions to help with her moving meltdown, as well as the assurance that we would be praying for her.

- Pray for God's peace in the midst of your chaos.
- Actively seek some help. You can't manage all that's on your plate alone.
- Communicate your needs to your husband. When he's home, he can give you a break to get away from the house for a while.
- Slow down, take a deep breath, and prioritize each day. What is the most important thing to do today?
- Rest when you can. Exhaustion distorts our perspective and outlook.

Bloom from Within

As an uprooted woman, you are similar to a daffodil bulb. When a daffodil bulb is planted, it is dormant for a season until it becomes rooted in the soil. Then sprouts begin to appear above the soil, the plant continues to grow, and finally it begins to bloom. I've had so many women tell me it seems to take a while before they put down roots in a community and begin to bloom. I know it took me a while after each move before I felt like myself again.

I suspect that during this move, you've given priority to everyone else in your family. You may feel you're lying dormant or that any new sprouts are pretty wilted. Let's pick off the wilted sprouts and give *you* the opportunity to grow and bloom.

Just as beautiful bouquets can be made up of a variety of flowers, so new friendships and connections can be seen as a lovely bouquet of unique and varied people. You bring to your world something no one else can. Your presence matters and adds beauty to life's bouquets! See if you can find yourself in one of the descriptions below and embrace your part of the bouquet!

- The daisy—She mixes well and is usually found in groups.
- The zinnia—Everybody knows her because she's dependable.
- The forget-me-not—She's so delicate; you won't forget her!
- The rose—So popular with everyone.
- The petunia—Extremely versatile and multitalented.
- The pansy—She has a cheerful and uplifting face.
- The impatiens—Guess you've figured her out! She's not content to be idle.
- The azalea—She brings maturity and grace with her presence.
- The begonia—Fits in anywhere she lives.
- The geranium—She adds so much color to a group.
- The tulip—Shy and might close up if not handled carefully.

You see, it takes all kinds of women, as well as all kinds of flowers, to make a beautiful garden bouquet. Each one adds her own fragrance, her own uniqueness, and her own beauty. Someone once said, "Who we are is God's gift to us. Who we *become* is our gift to God." I want to help you *become*—and begin to bloom from within!

Bloom through the fragrance of your life. "God . . . manifests through us the sweet aroma of the knowledge of Him in every place. For we are a fragrance of Christ to God" (2 Corinthians 2:14-15). Have you ever walked through the perfume section of a department store and found yourself drawn to the aroma of a certain fragrance? When you are a fragrance of Christ, people will be drawn to you. What will make you different in your community is not that you are new in town but that the fragrance of Christ permeates your surroundings. You will be known not only by how you bloom, but by the sweet aroma of His fragrance that you wear.

Bloom through your uniqueness. "You made all the delicate, inner parts of my body and knit them together in my mother's womb. Thank you for making me so wonderfully complex! . . . Your workmanship is marvelous—and how well I know it" (Psalm 139:13-14, TLB). Isn't it great to know you are not made with a cookie cutter? You are an original! That's the very best reason to be yourself, love yourself, and be good to yourself. God made you unique because He wanted your bloom to be one of a kind, unique from all the others.

Bloom through your beauty. "One thing . . . I shall seek: . . . to behold the beauty of the LORD" (Psalm 27:4). Christ is the creator of all beauty, both inside and outside.

A few "insider" beauty tips worth remembering:

- Your outer beauty is only skin-deep.
- It's the beauty from within that radiates in your life and makes you beautiful.
- I would rather see your heart than your hairstyle.
- I'm attracted to what matters to you—your thoughts and values—rather than your appearance.
- It is the indwelling beauty of Christ in your heart that allows your outer beauty to bloom.

It takes each person with her own fragrance, uniqueness, and beauty to make a lovely bouquet from the garden. You are, in essence, God's bouquet to the world around you. With that in mind, there are two more things I want you to do—celebrate who you are as you bloom from within. You are a daughter of the King! A child of God!

 ## Heart to Heart

Across the long driveway to my grandmother's house grew a magnificent, glorious wisteria vine with long purple flowers that looked like grape clusters. Wisteria vines are strong and sturdy, and they usually twine around trees, fences, or porch roofs. This particular one wrapped around a large oak tree. My cousins and I would pull loose one of the vines and swing across the driveway from a perch in the old oak tree. We got hours of entertainment out of that vine.

The memory of that wisteria vine lingers even after some sixty years. It carries a special meaning for me the older I get. The vine that wrapped around the oak tree is like God's love wrapped around me. The wisteria vine had become so strong and sturdy with time that nothing could disentangle it from the oak tree. Similarly, God's love is so strong and sturdy that nothing can separate His love from me.

That wonderful dangling vine that held me as I would swing across the driveway is much like God's arms that have carried me across many miles of life. He has held me through the good times and the hard times and many life changes. I pray that you, too, will feel God's love wrapped around you and His arms holding you close as you face change and transition in life.

Unpack Your Survival Box

Thirty practical and fun ways to help you "bloom":

1. Eat healthy foods . . . you've just got to do it.
2. Exercise whether you want to or not . . . good for your body, mind, and emotions.
3. Take vitamins . . . like a good girl should.
4. Treat yourself to a funky flavored ice-cream cone . . . just for the fun of it.
5. Lose yourself . . . in a good book.
6. Splurge and get a manicure or a pedicure . . . or both.
7. Go window-shopping . . . smile at your reflection in the glass.
8. Try one new thing each day.
9. Don't compare.
10. Be just who you are . . . and you will be wonderful.
11. Enjoy a free makeover at a department store, but remember it's only skin-deep.
12. Stop and smell the perfume. Be reminded that *your* fragrance of Christ will last.
13. When you meet someone for the first time, look her in the eyes and give her a firm handshake and a smile.
14. Focus on being rather than doing.

15. Seize the day!
16. Look up, not down; it really helps put life in perspective.
17. Buy something wonderful and frivolous for yourself.
18. Don't feel like you have to be productive all the time . . . learn to relax.
19. Pay it forward and buy the person behind you a cup of coffee.
20. Give yourself permission to cry if you want to—you'll just feel better if you do.
21. Visit a museum or an art gallery to appreciate the beauty of someone's masterpiece.
22. Remember *you* are God's masterpiece.
23. Treat yourself to a gourmet cup of flavored coffee or exotic herb tea, and savor each sip.
24. Take a class in something to expand your interests.
25. Go to a park that has playground equipment and swing. Be a kid again!
26. Walk as much as you can.
27. Buy a mixed bouquet of flowers, then give them to someone.
28. Have a grateful heart . . . and attitude.
29. Count your blessings every day.
30. Say your prayers every night.

Did you know that loneliness and loss of identity are the two leading responses from newcomers when they are asked, "What was the hardest thing about your move?" In the next two chapters, we'll talk about both of these issues!

CHAPTER 10

A PLACE IN YOUR HEART
CALLED LONELINESS

I lie awake, lonely as a solitary sparrow on the roof.
PSALM 102:7, TLB

THEIR DREAM HAD COME TRUE. Julie's husband had been accepted at graduate school. They were young, ready for new challenges, and eager for the opportunity to be near Julie's family on the West Coast. Everything had fallen into place just as they had planned, and they looked forward to this move.

They found a small cottage to rent near campus, and Julie got a teaching job. But soon, after the newness wore off, loneliness set in. Julie began to dislike everything about the new place where they lived. She had come from a small town in South Carolina to a big city in California. She felt isolated and lonely.

"Everyone is so busy," she said with discouragement in her voice. "It's so hard to get close to people. I feel like there isn't anyone who really knows me, or anyone I really know. The hardest thing about moving is being alone and not having a good friend to call and talk to. My husband and I are very close, but feeling so alone has caused conflict between us at times."

At first, Elaine was excited about moving and serving with her husband in ministry. She soon found that being a pastor's wife was a very lonely road to walk. "Everyone expected me to jump in immediately, start serving in everything and on every committee—and know everyone by name. I had all these people around me, yet I felt so alone. I yearned for a close friend who called me by name, rather than 'the pastor's wife.'"

A year later she was still feeling lonely. "I guess because I'm a pastor's wife, everyone wants to be my friend, but I still haven't found that special person I can feel safe with and trust completely to share my heart."

Melinda's loneliness from moving was bad enough, but it was compounded when her husband started traveling immediately after their move. He was usually gone Monday through Friday. She was shy, quiet, and not an initiator. "I feel like I'm on the outside of a sliding-glass door looking in, and nobody stops to open the door and ask me if I want to come in," Melinda said as she gazed off into the distance. Besides everything else, the couple's children were grown and married. "It's depressing to be so lonely," Melinda confessed.

Julie, Elaine, and Melinda have all felt the pain of loneliness and isolation that comes as a result of moving. Their stories are not unique.

Because nearly thirty-six million Americans move each year,[1] the feelings of loneliness and being disconnected from friends, family, and community are widespread.

In *A Nation of Strangers*, Vance Packard states,

We are seeing a sharp increase of people suffering alienation or just feeling adrift, which is having an impact on emotional and even physical health. We know there is a substantial increase of inhabitants suffering a loss of sense of community, identity, and continuity. These losses all contribute to a deteriorating sense of well-being, both for individuals and for society. In all this disruption of familiar patterns, some people respond with a deepened sense of loneliness.[2]

Many of us live in houses where we enter by pushing a button on the garage-door opener. The garage door opens and we drive in, then push the button again to close the door behind us. Our yards have six-foot privacy fences or concrete walls, preventing us from connecting with our neighbors. Any social contact happens not by coincidence but by effort. Not only has our mobility left us disconnected; it has left us rootless.

When you first move, the only one who calls you by name is the grocery store clerk who reads it on the receipt. Otherwise, you're an account number at the bank or a credit card at the mall.

One of my moving friends said that she looked forward to someone calling the wrong number, or even getting a solicitor's call, just to hear the phone ring.

According to *Merriam-Webster's Dictionary*, loneliness is the feeling of being "isolated; unhappy at being alone; longing for friends." Another definition says that loneliness is the emotional pain caused by social or emotional isolation from intimate relationships. *Our mobile society has certainly contributed to the loneliness of millions of people.*

Gilligan's Island

In his book *God, I've Got a Problem*, Ben Ferguson relates loneliness to the classic television series *Gilligan's Island*. In this classic hit of the 1960s, several castaways are marooned on an island, isolated from the rest of the world. Frantically, they send out distress signals and wave madly to passing ships in the hope that someone will rescue them from their plight.[3]

At times you've probably felt that no one saw your frantic distress signals as they passed by your island of loneliness. You were left alone without anyone slowing down or looking your way. All you could do was hope that eventually someone would see you or hear your cry.

In a Whisper

Judy, a newcomer to Phoenix, told me the story of how she had been rescued from her island of loneliness.

"The second day we moved here," Judy said, "I was running errands in a borrowed car. It was a typical August afternoon in Phoenix, with the temperature over 110 degrees. We had sold both of our cars in Maryland and had borrowed a car until we could buy one. The borrowed car had a lot of broken gauges, and the windows and wipers didn't work, but the air-conditioner did work, so I was fine.

"While I was out gathering things to set up the house, the car stalled in a major intersection. I didn't have any idea where to get help and knew no one to call. My husband couldn't come get me because we had only that one car. Finally, some people stopped and pushed my car out of the intersection and into the shade near a gas station. They could see I was really frazzled. I walked over to the station and got some gas, hoping it was only a broken gas gauge.

"I held back my tears until I got home, then went to my bedroom, closed the door, and sobbed. I cried out in anger and frustration at God (there was no point in yelling at my husband or children). 'How could you send me here? I can't find anything. I can't even find a gas station!' I ranted and raved for a while, repeating, 'I can't find anything. I can't find anything.' The tears stopped and I stretched out across the bed exhausted. It was then that I heard God's words so clearly in my head: *'You can always find Me.'* I realized in that moment what really mattered. Christ is with me everywhere I go. I'm never really alone. He didn't promise me I would always be happy, but He did promise He would always be with me."

As Judy cried out in distress, God reassured her of His presence. She felt His comfort easing the ache of loneliness in her heart. Something else of great significance happened as well. Even in the midst of the pain of loneliness, Judy heard God speaking to her. He spoke in what seemed like a whisper. If she had not been still and quiet, she would not have heard the words that brought her His reassurance and comfort.

Elijah, a great prophet in the Old Testament, had times in his life when he, too, felt overwhelmed by loneliness, and discouraged by his circumstances. (You can read his story in 1 Kings 19.) He became tired, isolated, and lonely, and began to lose perspective on life. When a move leaves you physically and emotionally worn-out and feeling isolated and lonely, you can lose perspective too.

"Go out and stand before me on the mountain," the Lord told him. And as Elijah stood there the Lord passed by, and a mighty windstorm hit the mountain; . . . but the Lord was not in the wind. After the wind, there was an earthquake, but the Lord was not in the earthquake. And after the earthquake, there was a fire, but the Lord was not in the fire. And after the fire, there was the sound of a gentle whisper.

I KINGS 19:11-12, TLB

That's when the Lord spoke to Elijah.

God didn't speak to Elijah through the clamor and chaos of the big things that were happening. He spoke in the quietness of a still, small voice—a gentle whisper. "Be still, and know that I am God" (Psalm 46:10, KJV).

 ## Heart to Heart

Are you listening for God's voice? What is He whispering to you in your loneliness? Could He be saying, *Come closer to Me, so you can hear Me?*

How can you hear God speak if you are isolated from Him or if you have chosen to separate from Him? "Draw near to God and He will draw near to you" (James 4:8).

My prayer for you at this very moment is that the loneliness you feel from this move will become the vehicle that drives you to Jesus Christ. I want you to have the pleasure of His company in your loneliness.

Have you ever felt lonely . . .

. . . in a room filled with friends?
. . . in a long, dark hospital corridor?
. . . in a beautiful new home?
. . . in a crowded mall?

... during the holidays?
... at church?
... at a party full of people?
... at a Bible study?
... as a newcomer to your community?

I have, and I know the pain of feeling disconnected from everyone. I've felt the emptiness that aches inside and the isolation that leaves me numb. I've been lonely, but I've never been alone. My relationship with Christ and His presence in my life sustain me. I have the pleasure of His company.

Cheryl, from Tennessee, writes: "Jesus knew personally the pain we sometimes encounter when leaving loved ones behind. At His crucifixion, He knew Mary and John would face loneliness living in a world suddenly void of His presence. Jesus gave them each other for emotional and spiritual support. Providing a new family for His loved ones was a high priority. Jesus promises that no one who has left home, brothers, sisters, mother, father, children, or field for His sake will fail to receive a hundred times as much in this present age (see Mark 10:29-30). What a comforting promise as I look up from my kitchen table over a new land to which He's brought us. Leaving loved ones still left us with a minor case of broken hearts, but the Great Physician has created both comfort and cure: a new family of friends that soothes our spirits and heals our hearts."

Lifelines for the Lonely

Remember the luggage tags in chapter 7? Loneliness may be one of the emotional tags you are wearing; you may find you're consumed with it. It may be the hardest thing you're dealing with in your move.

It was a comfort to me to know that Jesus has been to lonely places too. I've discovered on my journey that there really aren't any emotional places I've been, or feelings I've had, that Jesus hasn't experienced.

Jesus Himself would often slip away to the wilderness and pray.
LUKE 5:16

In her book *My Heart's Cry*, Anne Graham Lotz asks and answers the question, "Does your loneliness stem from the fact that you feel unknown? Or misunderstood? Or ignored? Then you need Jesus—and you need more of His nearness in your loneliness, because Jesus knows you, He understands you, and you have His undivided attention."[4]

If we were sitting on my porch, I would share with you some of the things that became a lifeline in my loneliness:

Refocus on God. Take your eyes off yourself and turn your eyes to Jesus. It's easy to lose focus on what's most important—God—instead of looking at your circumstances. We focus on filling our lives with people, things, or activities to escape from loneliness. The emptiness you feel should first be filled by God; then He will bring the right people and activities into your life to ease the loneliness.

Augustine said that there is a God-shaped vacuum in all of us that only He can fill. How are you filling your vacuum? Take this lonely time after a move to focus on His Word. Look to Him to fill all the lonely places and spaces in your heart and mind. Through this, you will begin to build a deeper relationship with God. Then you will come out the other side of loneliness a stronger, more confident, and fulfilled woman.

> As the deer pants for water, so I long for you, O God. I thirst for God, the living God. When can I find him to come and stand before him?
>
> PSALM 42:1-2, TLB

Listen to God. C. S. Lewis wrote, "God whispers to us in our pleasures, speaks in our conscience, but shouts in our pains. It is his megaphone to rouse a deaf world."[5] God may be using this move and the pain of your loneliness to get your full attention and draw you closer to Him. Listen . . . what is God trying to tell you?

• You will always have His presence with you. "I am with you always, even to the end of the age" (Matthew 28:20).

- You will feel joy and peace again. "I pray that God, the source of hope, will fill you completely with joy and peace because you trust in him" (Romans 15:13, NLT).
- You will be comforted. "When my worry is great within me, Your comfort brings joy to my soul" (Psalm 94:19, NLV).
- There is hope for tomorrow. "We who have turned to Him can have great comfort knowing that He will do what He has promised" (Hebrews 6:18, NLV).

There have been many times when loneliness overwhelmed me and I was so busy interpreting all the events of my life that I didn't hear what God was saying about the situation. Don't miss the moment. When God takes the time to whisper—or shout—you need to listen.

Talk to God. There's nothing like a good old one-on-one conversation with Jesus! Eyes wide open or closed, head bowed or looking straight ahead. Pray silently or speak aloud.

I talk out loud to Jesus just as I do with a best friend—because that's what He is. Anywhere, anytime works for me. My prayers are mostly out of gratitude because He's blessed me in countless ways. Praying for other people is good for my soul. It gets my focus off of myself, my loneliness without Bill, and what I think I need. It's a relief to know I can be honest, tell Jesus how I really feel, and know He still loves me. And guess what? If I take a deep breath every now and then, I can catch His response.

"Pray at all times as the Holy Spirit leads you to pray. Pray for the things that are needed. You must watch and keep on praying" (Ephesians 6:18, NLV).

Rest in God. I have often thought that the only time I'm not too busy, too scheduled, and too committed is after I move. For many of us, that pocket of time is like a clock that's waiting to be wound up. Until our life starts ticking again, we should take that time to rest; yet we often waste it by being frantic about our loneliness.

I'm a people person, but my effectiveness in giving and doing things for others is in direct proportion to the rest, solitude, and quiet time I spend with my Lord. I learned this lesson the hard way.

There was a time when I poured myself out to others without first being filled up through resting in—and being with—God. I ended up running on empty. Take this pocket of time God has given you and rest in His promises, rest in worship music, rest in His comfort and care. God is your refuge.

His arms are big enough to hold you for as long as you need to rest in Him. "Come to Me, all who are weary and heavy-laden, and I will give you rest" (Matthew 11:28).

Wait on God. It's hard to wait, isn't it? You may already be tired of:

- waiting to fit in,
- waiting to make friends,
- waiting to feel at home,
- waiting to be included,
- waiting to be accepted,
- *waiting for the loneliness to go away.*

Waiting on God is hard sometimes. We don't understand why we have to wait so long for all the pieces of life to come together again. Trust me, the pieces will come together—in God's timing, not ours. But it's during the waiting, during the space between now and then, that much is learned. God's waiting room is not a bad place to be. While I waited, He taught me about *trust* and a whole lot about *patience.* So many times, I tried to figure everything out myself, but it just didn't work that way. I only became anxious, unhappy, and miserable. I had many pity parties in my loneliness, and I didn't know anyone to invite to join me! Trust God in all things, take a deep breath, and practice patience every day.

The apostle Paul knew about waiting. He suffered the anguish of loneliness in prison. Instead of feeling sorry for himself, though, he studied and prepared for the day he would be released (see 2 Timothy 4:13). As you wait on God, what are you doing to be ready for the day you are released from your prison of loneliness?

Reach out to others. Are you waiting for other people to reach out to you in your loneliness? Many times after a move, I've dreamed of neighbors knocking on my door to welcome me into the neighborhood. I've imagined them bringing me flowers, a fresh-baked pie or brownies, and a list of places to go and things to do. You know, like a good neighbor would do in a minute! For all the times people have reached out to me, there have been just as many times they haven't. I can choose to feel sorry for myself and indulge in a lot of self-pity. But that's not the answer. The answer is to stop thinking about me and start thinking about them.

Joan, a moving friend, offered good advice for newcomers. She said, "Reach out to others. There are plenty of people who are a lot more needy than we are." Who knows, they could even be your neighbors. So I have learned to pursue others, to make it happen, to jump in, to just do it. That's not easy for shy women to do, but it's one of the conditions of being a mover. You've just got to grit your teeth and take the first step.

One of the joys in my life has been to see newcomers reaching out to other newcomers in our church through our Moving On After Moving In group. They get it. They've experienced it.

I see these women embrace each other, take meals to each other, hold hands and pray together, grieve together, grow together in Christ, take care of each other's children, cry together, make hospital visits, help each other with tasks, laugh together, and heal together. Their loneliness is filled with Jesus and each other! "Treat others the same way you want them to treat you" (Luke 6:31).

In Elisabeth Elliot's book *Loneliness,* she writes, "The answer to our loneliness is *love*—not our finding someone to love us, but our surrendering to the God who has always loved us with an everlasting love. Loving Him is then expressed in a happy and full-hearted pouring out of ourselves in love to others."[6]

These are the things I want to share with you as we sit on my porch. Tuck them into the lonely places of your heart. And remember that God has not forgotten you.

Unpack Your Survival Box

This chapter dealt mostly with matters of the heart. Now let's balance those matters with things you can *do* to help alleviate loneliness:

- One moving friend wrote that she started a home business selling jewelry when she moved to a new place. She had neighborhood home parties, and they helped her meet people quickly!
- A newcomer had all the contractors (and their wives) who built her new home over for an appreciation dinner!
- Hit the garage sales on Friday and Saturday mornings. You can learn your way around your new town and have fun doing it.
- Find a hobby or something creative you can do or learn that involves others: art classes, hiking groups, a book club, etc.
- Find a Christian bookstore in town. Skim through the books to choose one that will encourage your heart and deepen your growth in Christ. Buy some praise and worship music that makes you smile.
- Sign up to be a greeter at church.
- Volunteer your home for school meetings, neighborhood meetings, and church meetings.
- Check the paper or the web for fun places to go or new things to see.
- If you have kids in school, see if there is a Moms in Prayer group in your area.
- Volunteer to help out with any community fund-raiser in your neighborhood.
- Don't substitute electronic communication for face-to-face contact.
- Have your own neighborhood coffee! Personally deliver the invitations or put them on neighbors' doors.
- Don't feel sorry for yourself. Remember, "This too shall pass."

According to the responses to my questionnaire, the second-hardest thing about moving is loss of identity. A moving friend told me once that she had moved so many times she didn't know *where* she was, much less *who* she was! So in the next chapter, let's find out who you really are.

NOBODY KNOWS MY NAME

"Who are you?" said the Caterpillar.

*Alice replied, rather shyly, "I–I hardly know, Sir,
just at present—at least I know who I was when I got
up this morning, but I think I must have been changed
several times since then."*

LEWIS CARROLL, *Alice's Adventures in Wonderland*

THE LOSS-OF-SELF EXPERIENCE resonates with thousands of uprooted women.

"Tears come as I think back to the first year of transition here in this new town," Marian wrote. "I made so many sacrifices in this move, but the greatest was my immediate and devastating loss of identity. Here I was, in the midst of the desert with nothing, truly nothing. I had been stripped of the roles I had played: wife of the successful corporate executive, keeper of the lovely home, busy and involved mom of four, and loyal friend with meaningful relationships. Plus, I didn't even know how to get to the grocery store or anywhere else I needed to go."

Sound familiar? Marian's words could easily read like a neon banner that you might wear: "Fragile, Identity Lost in Move."

You've moved from those who know you best to those who don't know you at all.

There is an echo of emptiness in your heart, a feeling of being invisible to those around you.

Lost: My Credentials

I shared with you earlier how the biggest luggage tag I wore when I moved was one that read "Loss of Identity." That was the most difficult personal struggle I had to face in my effort to start over. I really felt like I'd lost myself in one of the many moving boxes still in the garage. Nobody knew my name, much less who I was. I wanted to wear a sign around my neck saying, "My name is Susan. I'm friendly. I love lattes and country music and I have an adventurous spirit. You would like me! Please talk to me."

It may sound silly, but I was desperate. As a new woman in the community, I didn't have any history there. I had a basic need to be known, accepted, and loved in my new world, yet nobody knew me well enough to accept me or to love me. I wanted instant results, but establishing community takes time.

In my desperation to belong, I tried to fit in by being someone I wasn't. I tried to be athletic and play tennis like everyone else but failed miserably. I tried to wear cute Western-style clothes but didn't have the figure and felt foolish.

I felt inadequate in my new surroundings. I sank further into despair as my self-esteem went downhill and stayed there. I asked myself, *What's happening to me? Where is that confident person I once was? What happened to the person who knew who she was and felt like she had it all together? Why can't I get a grip on life?*

I prayed for the strength to overcome my feelings. I cried out to God to help me rise above the emotions. But God had me right where He wanted me—in a place of total dependence on Him. *God used my loss of identity to create a desire to turn to Him to quench my thirsty soul.* He was my only oasis. My emotional survival was dependent on Him alone.

The loss of identity I felt in moving is echoed in the voices of movers everywhere.

Alma had been in school working on her PhD while living in Colorado. Her identity was wrapped up in being a full-time graduate student. When she and her family moved, she had to drop out of her

NOBODY KNOWS MY NAME || 121

program. "I was pushed out of my comfort zone, and I didn't know who I was or how to act. What was my role? I had lost my identity."

The good news is that Alma says the move was exactly what her life needed. She and her husband started attending a church where they began to grow in Christ, and they haven't stopped growing since. She found a new identity—as a Bible study teacher and leader in church.

After her move from South Carolina to California, Julie said, "I felt like a social outcast from the South. No one bothered to get to know me or talk to me. I kept thinking that something must be wrong with me or people would like me."

The good news is that God gave Julie the courage to do some volunteer work in the community, and she met other people who enjoyed doing the same thing. She became confident in her new role as a volunteer. She said, "I just kept forcing myself to reach out to others, even though it wasn't always easy."

When Allicia moved to Florida, she nearly drowned in her self-pity. She said, "Being new, you always feel like you have to 'sell yourself.' Other people have to make room in their lives for you. I would ask myself, 'Am I worthy enough for them to make room for me?'"

The good news about Allicia's story is that God profoundly changed her life. His Word penetrated her heart and she came to know Jesus Christ. She no longer lived in self-pity but in the confidence of who she was in Christ.

Judy moved from her hometown in Maryland. She didn't hesitate when she told me, "Every time I move, I have an identity crisis. I question, *Will people like me?* I wonder what to reveal about myself and what to hide. I'm often guarded and edgy about what I say or don't say. I'm uncomfortable with having to explain myself over and over because I don't know if they even care."

Judy's good news: "This move, I've made a conscious effort to depend on God to meet all my needs. I don't want to be dependent on my husband, on other people, or on things to fill my identity. When I'm lonely, I talk to Jesus. When I'm frustrated, I talk to Jesus. When I need a friend to share my insecurities, I talk to Jesus. Who better than Jesus would know

122 || AFTER THE BOXES ARE UNPACKED

what it's like to leave a home He loves, to come to an unknown, new place?" Then she said, "I wonder if Jesus ever got homesick for heaven?"

Patty's tenth move was to Ohio. "I have to start building my self-confidence all over again. I'm back at square one." Some months later I heard from Patty again. Her good news: "I reminded myself that God didn't bring us here to go backward. So many of the pieces still haven't fallen into place, but God has my complete attention. I'm spending more time in prayer than I ever have. I'm convinced that He's doing something in me that couldn't have happened unless I had gotten back to square one."

These women may have lost their credentials, but they found their identities in Christ. Do you feel like you've experienced an identity crisis? Let's take a further look in all the right places, not only to find your credentials but your true identity.

Mirror, Mirror on the Wall, Who's the Most Insecure of All?

Sometimes I dread those three-way mirrors in department stores. They can plunge me into reality more quickly than anything else. They tell me far more than I want to know. Not only can I see myself from head to toe, but I can see side and back views. Nothing is hidden; it's all staring back at me, especially when I'm trying on bathing suits. Talk about loss of identity! Any thoughts I may have had about my body looking like those magazine ads are just an illusion when I look in that mirror. (I know you're smiling, because you've looked in that same mirror, haven't you?)

Let's step in front of an imaginary full-length, three-way mirror and take a good look at ourselves. You get a quick overview from head to toe—a front, side, and back view. It tells you if you're coordinated, if you look all together, and if you have on shoes and earrings that match. (I've been known to show up with one black and one blue shoe!) A three-way mirror at the department store only tells you how you look on the outside. You might need to take a closer look on the *inside* as well as the outside from the following three views as you size up how you are doing since your move:

Physically. How do you look since you moved? Do you look tired? Have you gained a few extra pounds? (It happens, believe me!) Do you need a haircut? Do your clothes fit the style and the climate of your new area? *What do you see about yourself that needs some personal care?*

Spiritually. Take a look at your relationship with God. Are you angry with Him? Do you feel close to Him, or are you disconnected from Him? Do you really even know who God is? *How are you doing spiritually?*

Emotionally. Take a look at how you're feeling. Do you feel like you're stuck in a mire of emotions, or are you beginning to get a grip? Have you worked through any feelings you're struggling with? Do you find yourself an emotional wreck all the time? *What emotions are you dealing with?*

A *magnifying mirror* may be small, but it shows everything in a BIG way. A magnifying mirror gives you a closer look at who you are. You can even see more clearly the unresolved issues of your heart. It allows you to see your blemishes so you know what action to take to correct them. It also gives you a really close look at what needs to be improved and what changes need to be made in your attitude or your outlook. It's wise to take a magnified look at yourself.

When you take the time to look closely, are there some changes that need to be made?

Oh yes, and I shouldn't forget the *distorted* mirror. You usually find those at an amusement park, a circus, or the fair. I always laugh when I see myself in a distorted mirror. It reflects an unrealistic view of who I am. At times, it's easy to have a distorted view of yourself, especially when you're trying to be someone you're not. It's hard to see who you really are when you base your image on false or negative perceptions. *Remember, you are made in the image of God, not in the image of a distorted perception.*

I left the best for last. There's one more mirror I want you to see. Let's call it the *true reflection mirror.* It reflects how Jesus sees you, not how you see yourself. It's a mirror that reflects a changed heart, and it is wiped clean every day with God's forgiveness.

You look at the *outside* and see all the things you think are wrong about you. Jesus looks at the *inside* and sees all the things right about you. "He has brought you into his own presence, and you are holy and blameless as you stand before him without a single fault" (Colossians 1:22, NLT).

Do this for me: The next time you look in a mirror, imagine that Jesus is standing by your side, looking in the mirror with you.

- He is smiling because you are precious in His sight (Isaiah 43:4).
- He loves you more than life itself (John 3:16).
- He sees you with eyes of acceptance (Romans 15:7).
- He values you with all His heart (Matthew 10:31).
- Through Him, you are forgiven (Nehemiah 9:17).

Now we see things imperfectly, like puzzling reflections in a mirror, but then we will see everything with perfect clarity. All that I know now is partial and incomplete, but then I will know everything completely, just as God now knows me completely.

I CORINTHIANS 13:12, NLT

Take a good look at the *true reflection mirror* every day!

Found: My Identity

The world would have you believe your identity is found through other people, commercials, television, magazines, books, and advertisements. *Your true identity is found in Christ, not in your appearance, your performance, or your status.* There's nothing wrong with looking your best, doing your best, and becoming your best. But don't make the mistake of wrapping your identity in those things. Believe me, your appearance, your performance, and even your status come and go in life. They are not who you are. Only in Christ will you find your security and significance. Only in Christ will you find your true identity. Only in Him will you feel totally complete.

May you "know the love of Christ which surpasses knowledge, that you may be filled up to all the fullness of God" (Ephesians 3:19).

I can't help but think of the story of the woman at the well (see John 4:1-30). Oh, wow; talk about finding her identity! She was spiritually lost—then found, with the help of Jesus. She isn't even referred to by name, only as "the Samaritan woman." I imagine her appearance was that of a woman who was used to many treks to the deep well to fill her water jar. Her clothes were probably somewhat frayed and smudged with dirt. She had been married five times and, at this point, was living a promiscuous lifestyle. Most likely, all of this would have served to form her identity.

Then she encounters Jesus. He asks for a drink of water, strikes up a conversation, and the conversation changes her life forever.

> He replied, "If you only knew what a wonderful gift God has for you, and who I am, you would ask me for some *living* water!" . . .
>
> "Please, sir," the woman said, "give me some of that water! Then I'll never be thirsty again." . . .
>
> The woman left her waterpot beside the well and went back to the village and told everyone, "Come and meet a man who told me everything I ever did!"
>
> JOHN 4:10,15,28-29, TLB

The Samaritan woman needed unconditional love and acceptance. She was looking for security and significance. She wanted to belong somewhere or to someone. Yet she wasn't called by name and no one cared to know everything about her—until Jesus entered her life.

Can you relate?

You want to be loved and accepted by new friends. You're looking for security and significance in a new place. You want so much to belong in the community. Yet no one knows your name. No one knows your story. You're known only as "the new woman who just moved here."

When the need to be known isn't met, the result is too often a loss of identity, self-esteem, or self-image. That's why it's so vital for us to know who we are in Christ. *Our security is in knowing we belong to Jesus. Our significance is found in Him.* He knows our name. He knows our story. He loves us unconditionally and accepts us—no matter who we are or where we are!

I have found my identity, as did the woman at the well. Have you? Take a look at who you are in Christ.

You are His treasure! Sometimes you might not feel very special, or like anyone would think you are special. Listen up! In God's eyes, you shine and sparkle! Like a treasure chest full of jewels. He has *chosen* you . . . *you* . . . YOU to be His very own treasure—priceless and precious to Him.

> The LORD your God has chosen you to be his own special treasure.
>
> DEUTERONOMY 7:6, NLT

You are incredibly loved! God loves you unconditionally and His love for you never changes. Do you get it? *Unconditionally. Never changes.* Some of you have never experienced that kind of love. His love is not based on your performance. Isn't that a relief? One more thing to remember: Don't relate your circumstances to God's love for you. No matter what your circumstances are, God's love remains the same.

> I have loved you with an everlasting love.
>
> JEREMIAH 31:3

You are known inside and out! God knows everything about you. He knows you better than you know yourself. He even knows your dark side and your secrets. Nothing is hidden from Him.

> O LORD, You have searched me and known me.
>
> PSALM 139:1

You are accepted with no strings attached! God accepts you just as you are, in spite of your weaknesses, your failures, and your flaws—completely and unconditionally. You don't have to be perfect to be accepted. Pretty awesome, isn't it?

> Accept one another, just as Christ also accepted us to the
> glory of God.
>
> ROMANS 15:7

You are in process to become like Christ! God is working in you and through you as He conforms you to the image of Christ. It's a work in progress on every level of your life. Embrace it to the finish line!

> And I am sure that God who began the good work within you
> will keep right on helping you grow in his grace until his task
> within you is finally finished on that day when Jesus Christ
> returns.
>
> PHILIPPIANS 1:6, TLB

You are valued beyond measure! God cherishes you. He adopted you as a daughter. You are a member of His family forever. He sent Jesus Christ to earth to redeem you. You can have no greater value than that!

> See how great a love the Father has bestowed on us, that we
> would be called children of God; and such we are.
>
> 1 JOHN 3:1

You are designed by God and unique! No one else is like you! You are one of a kind. He has a special purpose for designing you just the way you are. He created you and continues to form and mold you through your circumstances.

> For You formed my inward parts; You wove me in my
> mother's womb. I will give thanks to You, for I am fearfully
> and wonderfully made.
>
> PSALM 139:13-14

You are made for a reason and a purpose! Our purpose in life is to know and please God. As we come to know God more intimately, we have a greater desire to please Him.

> Let them boast in this alone: That they truly know me, and understand that I am the Lord . . . whose love is steadfast.
>
> JEREMIAH 9:24, TLB

There is Someone who knows your name!

> Do not fear, for I have redeemed you; I have called you by name; you are Mine!
>
> ISAIAH 43:1

Remember Marian's quote at the beginning of this chapter? This is how she ended it: *"The loss of identity that crushed me is gradually reshaping me into the likeness of my dear Jesus."*

Heart to Heart

Let's have a good heart-to-heart for a minute. So many of you have said to me, "When I look in the mirror, I'm not sure who I really am anymore, and I don't even know how to begin finding out."

Listen, my friend, it doesn't matter how many mirrors you look into. Until you take your mask off, you can't see who you really are. Some of you have hidden behind a mask because it protects you from the anguish of a troubled marriage or a broken relationship. It could be a safe place to hide where you don't have to face the pain and heartache in your life. Maybe it's a cover-up for your loss of identity, your damaged self-image, or your fragile self-esteem.

Whatever the reason, I'm giving you permission to take off your mask now. Don't you see? When you know God loves you unconditionally, accepts you just as you are, values you above all else, knows everything about you, and will never, ever leave you, you can have the confidence to be the real you! What better time to become real than when you're starting over in a new place?

There's a wonderful freedom in taking off your mask and letting God's love penetrate your heart, warming you from the inside out. I know, because I took off my mask that covered up my low self-esteem and protected me from anyone knowing how inadequate I felt after we moved. If I can do it, so can you!

Margery Williams's charming children's book *The Velveteen Rabbit* shares this conversation between two friends in the nursery:

> "What is REAL?" asked the Rabbit. . . .
>
> "Real isn't how you are made," said the Skin Horse. "It's a thing that happens to you. When a child loves you for a long, long time, not just to play with, but REALLY loves you, then you become Real."
>
> "Does it hurt?" asked the Rabbit.
>
> "Sometimes," said the Skin Horse, for he was always truthful. "When you are Real, you don't mind being hurt."[1]

God has loved you, my friend, for a long, long time. REALLY loved you. Now *you* can become real as well.

In the next three chapters we'll talk about some subjects that are near and dear to our hearts: our husbands, our children, and our friends. What do a cake mix and a husband have in common? Read on.

CHAPTER 12

HAVE I TOLD YOU LATELY THAT I LOVE YOU?

Wherever you go, I will go; wherever you live, I will live.
RUTH 1:16, NLT

HAVE YOU ASKED YOURSELF, "How is this move affecting my marriage?"

This is what Teri shared with me about her marriage and moving: "Our move created an emotional distance between my husband and me. We were separated for three months while I stayed behind to sell the house and wait for the children to get out of school. We both got used to functioning independently. Neither of us felt we needed each other the way we had before the move. It took a couple of months for us to even begin to feel as if we were functioning as a couple and as a family again."

Teri is not alone in her feelings about her husband and their move. When I asked other women how moving had affected their marriages, they were eager to share both the positive and the negative. Here are some of their comments. See if you identify with any of them.

"We have always been extremely close, but we have had lots of conflict over my loneliness. He had to be everything for me."

"He became consumed with his work and I felt left out."

"Overall, I'd say it made us closer. At first, all we had was each other for companionship."

"Because of the instability of his new job, we drew closer together. Even though there was change all around us, our relationship was constant."

"We hadn't changed, and that familiarity felt good."

"The move created conflict at first, because I'd left a lot behind, but then the move brought us closer because we only had each other. Since my schedule had come to a standstill, I had more time to give, and less stress."

"We have been on an emotional roller coaster with six jobs in three years. It's been too many adjustments and has created a lot of problems."

"I felt resentful that nothing seemed to ruffle him."

"When I'm feeling sorry for myself, it's easy for me to blame my husband for my difficult circumstances. If I can see the situation with a sense of humor, it helps everything."

"I'm an Army wife who has moved nine times in twelve years of marriage. My husband has been deployed four times. The stress on our marriage is unimaginable. I don't know if I can handle the pressure on our relationship anymore."

Don't overlook how moving can affect your marriage. Many of you may have moved for your husband's job. You and your husband may be like two ships passing in the night, each one going in a different direction. You are preoccupied with all the tasks that need to be done before and after your move. He is preoccupied with his new job. The last thing the two of you are thinking about is the strain a move can have on your relationship. The more in sync you are with each other, the better your marriage can thrive during this stressful transition.

For many couples, the changes and adjustments of being uprooted bring their marriage relationship closer; for others it's just another brick in the wall between them. It is my hope that through this chapter, you will gain insight into how to move closer to each other, and that you will begin to build bridges instead of walls in your marriage.

Needless to say, our "marriage on the move" went through every phase and stage, every feeling and emotion—from heartache to happiness.

Me and My Moving Man

When Bill and I were dating, I remember telling him in a romantic voice, "I'll follow you to the ends of the earth!" After fourteen moves and forty-five years of marriage, I remember telling him that I still would!

When Bill chose hotel and restaurant management as a career, it seemed our address would always be changing. Since hotels are open twenty-four hours a day, 365 days a year, and their busiest restaurant times are holidays—guess who was left alone a lot? We faced the challenge of Bill's demanding long days at work, hit-and-miss dinnertimes together, and very little time together on the weekends and holidays.

There were seasons when I felt like I was a single mom trying to hold life together alone. We struggled with communicating after long hours of being apart, and the disconnection between us slowly became a wedge of silence. Not only was climbing the corporate ladder the catalyst for fourteen moves; it became the breaking point in our marriage. We were faced with a choice: let a career continue to drive us apart, or begin putting the pieces of "us" back together again.

We would not allow what had fractured us to shatter us.

Bottom line, we loved each other deeply and were committed to our marriage. But somewhere along the way, we lost sight of each other in the maze of career and children. We rededicated our commitment to a Christ-centered marriage, and to each other, at a marriage conference in Atlanta over thirty-five years ago.

As I look back over those early years of marriage and moving, it was the challenges that made me stronger, the struggles that made me more steadfast, and the breaking points that strengthened me. *But it was God, and only God, who healed our brokenness.*

At the bottom of one of my favorite pictures of Bill and me, taken many years ago, I placed this verse: "Now all glory to God, who is able, through his mighty power at work within us, to accomplish infinitely more than we might ask or think" (Ephesians 3:20, NLT). I claimed that verse of victory for our marriage. I readily admit that it was God who empowered our marriage far beyond all I could ever ask or think.

Don't Forget to Unpack Your Husband

I must admit, there were times when I wanted to pack Bill in a box and store him in the garage. And there were times when I was insensitive to his needs and emotions and forgot to unpack him in the move.

In order to unpack your husband, you've got to understand him. I've come up with four different types of husbands who move, based on my personal experience and what other uprooted women have told me.

All Work; No Play

- Goes to work early and stays late. Goes to the office on weekends.
- Brings work home.
- Will move every two to three years if necessary for his career.

The Jock

- Life is centered around playing or watching golf, tennis, or other sports.
- Checks out the teams in the area and the availability of the sport he wants to play before moving.
- Likes an excuse to buy the latest sports equipment.

The Computer Geek

- Spends hours on the computer and knows everything about technology.
- Will do in-depth research regarding the move.
- Has the latest technological gadgets.

The Clueless Optimist

- Thinks his wife is as happy about moving as he is.
- Believes moving will be a wonderful experience for everyone in the family.
- Doesn't understand why others struggle with the move.

You may identify some of these characteristics in your husband, or you may find that none of them apply to him. But zero in on the type of "moving man" you have so you can better *understand* him, not criticize him.

What do you do then?

Pray for him. Remember, you can't change your husband, but God can! Sometimes we run ahead of God and try to "fix" our husbands. Doesn't work. I know. On more than one occasion, I actually tried to be Bill's "Holy Nagging Spirit" and tell him everything I thought he was doing wrong in our marriage. God reminded me through His Word that I needed to stop talking and get out of the way. I needed to let God do what He does best and be the wife He designed me to be.

Follow the what, how, and when rule. It's not what you say but how you say it and when you say it. Too often we can lash out in anger or resentment. We say words that are hurtful and can't be taken back. On top of that, we choose the worst possible timing to discuss something. Pray about what you're going to say and when to say it.

Love him unconditionally. Sometimes we put conditions on our marriage without realizing that we're doing it. Simply love him. Show it with your eyes, your smile, your words, your touch. He'll know it, he'll feel it, and walls will begin to come down.

Accept him for who he is, not for who you want him to be. Acceptance comes with unconditional love. He may have a different personality or temperament than yours. Well, if God made us all alike, we wouldn't need each other. I'm an extrovert, and Bill was an introvert. I just knew Bill would have more fun in life if he was just like me! Yet he was my quiet, strong, and steady anchor. My fun-loving self needed him.

Forgive him. It might be the little hurts that have stacked up or the big hurts that have wedged between you as a result of your move. It could be something deeper, and moving was just the tip of the iceberg that began to freeze your emotions and your feelings. With forgiveness, healing and restoration can begin.

Over the years of our marriage, Bill would say that he had been several of these different types of men. He was All Work; No Play and a Clueless Optimist, as well as a few of the other characters.

I loved him then, and yes, even today he still holds my heart. God revealed in both our lives how to understand and love each other more fully. God blessed us, even through tough times, with forty-five years together. It just doesn't get much better than that.

What Do Your Husband and a Cake Mix Have in Common?

They both come with the basic ingredients in the box! Of course, you have to add additional ingredients to the mix and to your man. When you buy a cake mix at the store, a basic prepackaged mixture of flour, sugar, and cornstarch or baking powder comes in the box. You have to add the water, eggs, and butter or oil. Sometimes there's even pudding already added, which makes it really yummy. Then, to complete the cake, you stir in all the ingredients, bake it, and frost it.

When you get married, your husband also comes prepackaged with basic ingredients: genetic characteristics and personality, his family background and influences, and his life experiences. You add important ingredients such as acceptance, encouragement, appreciation, and respect. Then you add the frosting—love! Just as frosting covers the flaws and cracks in a cake, so love covers the flaws and cracks in your marriage. (Bet you'll think about your husband the next time you bake a cake!)

Since I'm all about how to live out God's Word, let's look at some practical dos and don'ts related to some key added ingredients.

Acceptance. You may not realize it, but you mirror your acceptance or disapproval with your body language. Expressing frustration with your face, crossing your arms, rolling your eyes, tapping your foot—all are negative responses. See his worth beyond his faults and mirror that.

Accept one another, just as Christ also accepted us to the
glory of God.
ROMANS 15:7

Encouragement. Be his cheerleader! Encourage him with praise
and affirmation to give him confidence and hope. He might need
some encouragement if things aren't going well at work or if he is discouraged about something. "You can do it!" and "I believe in you!" are
two of my favorite encouraging one-liners.

Encourage one another and build up one another, just as you
also are doing.
I THESSALONIANS 5:11

Appreciation. Tell him you appreciate something he did or said.
Write a note in a greeting card, Post-it note, e-mail, or text. At the right
moment, look him in the eye and *tell* him why you appreciate him.
Demonstrate your appreciation through a gesture or act of kindness.

Be thankful.
COLOSSIANS 3:15

Respect. One way to show respect is to build him up, not tear him
down, in front of family and friends. Also, you show respect when you
listen to his ideas and ask his opinion, even if you disagree.

Take delight in honoring each other.
ROMANS 12:10, TLB

Affection. I think of affection as an "observable love." It's love that
you can see, touch, and feel. You can see it expressed in kind and
thoughtful acts of love. You can feel it through a touch, a kiss, or a hug.
Affection is love lived out. Don't just say "I love you"—show it!

Love each other with genuine affection.
ROMANS 12:10, NLT

All of the things you add help you unpack your husband and strengthen your relationship after a move. They are also the ingredients that can give your marriage a new beginning.

Go Back to the Basics

Going back to God's Word is the basic foundation for your marriage. Let these verses be gentle reminders to blend in with all the ingredients you add.

> Not because we think we can do anything of lasting value by ourselves. Our only power and success comes from God.
>
> 2 CORINTHIANS 3:5, TLB

> Let us not lose heart in doing good, for in due time we will reap if we do not grow weary.
>
> GALATIANS 6:9

> Say only what is good and helpful to those you are talking to, and what will give them a blessing.
>
> EPHESIANS 4:29, TLB

> Let all bitterness and wrath and anger and clamor and slander be put away from you, along with all malice. Be kind to one another, tender-hearted, forgiving each other, just as God in Christ also has forgiven you.
>
> EPHESIANS 4:31-32

> Worry in the heart of a man weighs it down, but a good word makes it glad.
>
> PROVERBS 12:25, NLV

> Let us help each other to love others and to do good.
>
> HEBREWS 10:24, NLV

Whatever is true, whatever is honorable, whatever is right,
whatever is pure, whatever is lovely, whatever is of good
repute, if there is any excellence and if anything worthy
of praise, dwell on these things.

PHILIPPIANS 4:8

A Letter from Don

I received this letter from the husband of my friend Marian in Colorado.
He wanted you to know some of the ways she supported him through
the moving process. It offers great insight from a man's perspective:

Marian encouraged me by her selfless giving to God's greater
purpose and by unconditionally giving of herself to our
children and to me. She is a model mom. Through her gifts
of wisdom and organization, she provides the priorities and
focus for our family. She accepts her position as Mom by
ensuring that our children are growing spiritually, settled in
school, provided for at church, and comforted at home.

The trauma of moving is looked at nose-to-nose and
dealt with. Knowing that our children are more than
surviving gives me confidence and assurance. She watches
me and lovingly points out when I'm distracted by work,
grumpy with the kids, or neglecting our family.

She is a lighthouse, always helping me stay on course. She
rebukes me when I sometimes long to be back in Arizona.
She instills an eagerness in each of us to look for the blessing
in each situation. She listens and talks through the anguish of
new job adjustments. We recognize the difficulties, talk about
them, deal with them—and then move on to more fruitful
and pleasant times.

She talks about her own hopes and dreams. By having
the wisdom of discernment, Marian can recognize and define
hopes and opportunities. And, of course, all of this is possible
because of her commitment and loving relationship to Jesus.

She seeks. She prays. The pain and the remembrance of the pain of moving is sometimes wrenching. The blessing of new friends, new experiences, new learning, new opportunity is here; but we must reach out and take it. Marian is helping us do that.

Sincerely,

Don

Here are some ways to strengthen your marriage after a move (taken from my book *But Mom, I Don't Want to Move!*[1]).

- Start daily devotions and prayer times together.
- Pray for each other and give thanks for each other.
- Improve communication by having weekly catch-up conversations.
- Keep short accounts with each other.
- Schedule regular time for a date night.
- Learn each other's love languages. (See Gary Chapman's *The Five Love Languages*.)
- Plan a getaway for just the two of you.
- Look for the "stress cracks" in your spouse. (Is the job working out? Is everything coming together at home?)
- Be there for each other and let your children see that you are.

Heart to Heart

Think back to the time when you first fell in love with your husband. You chose him and committed your heart to him. Just knowing you loved him made your life wonderful. Every day with him was more special than the day before. You wore what you knew he would like and you never stopped smiling when you were together.

Then somewhere along the way, you became disappointed and disillusioned with him. Those special days became ordinary and mundane.

You were fairy tale–minded back then. You only had visions of living happily ever after. You forgot that even fairy tales include scenes of sorrow and hardship, disillusionment and disappointment. In real life, those struggles often continue on and on, making you think there won't ever be a happy ending.

Life is not always easy. No marriage is perfect. But you can choose to love your husband again, to entrust your heart to him again, and to find ways to revive those special moments together. Then you can whisper in his ear, "Have I told you lately that I love you?"

 ## Unpack Your Survival Box

Twenty-five ways to express your love for your husband:

1. Be his cheerleader—not his critic.
2. Greet him at the door when he comes home from work.
3. Bake his favorite dessert or make his favorite meal.
4. Write a love note and put it in his briefcase or coat pocket.
5. Frame a recent picture of yourself for his office.
6. Hold hands in public or at the movies.
7. Tell him you believe in him.
8. Listen to him.
9. Learn as much as you can about his work.
10. Always kiss him good-bye in the morning.
11. Always kiss him good night.
12. Call or text him at work and tell him you are thinking about him.
13. When he returns home from a trip, put a Welcome Home sign on the door.
14. Buy his favorite ice cream.
15. Mail a romantic card to him at his office.
16. Watch a game on TV with him.
17. Never criticize him in public and never compare him to someone else's husband.
18. Tell him you love him at least once a day.

19. A hug can speak volumes; so can a kiss.
20. Write "I love you" on the bathroom mirror with lipstick.
21. Plan a date night and go to his favorite restaurant.
22. Speak of his good qualities; pray about his bad qualities.
23. Anticipate his needs.
24. Look him in the eyes and say, "I'd follow you to the ends of the earth."
25. Tell him five reasons you would move anywhere with him.

How do you help your children adjust to a move? Lots of helpful ideas are coming up next!

CHAPTER 13

ROOTS AND WINGS

There are only two lasting bequests we can hope to give our children. One of these is roots, the other, wings.
JOHANN WOLFGANG VON GOETHE

"MAMA, I HAVE SOME NEWS," I said apprehensively. "We're moving again. Pretty far away this time."

I dreaded her response. I knew my mother's words would affect me and either encourage or discourage my feelings about the move.

"Where are you going?"

"To the other side of the world—Phoenix, Arizona! Bill has a wonderful opportunity with the corporate office. His company is flying us out there in a couple of weeks to look for a house."

I will never forget the first words Mama spoke. "Oh, Susan," she said with excitement in her voice, "that's wonderful! I've always wanted to go to Phoenix. Now I'll have a reason to see that part of the country!"

Her positive response not only gave me the encouragement I wanted and needed, but there were no strings of guilt attached to my leaving. There was a healthy freeing up in my heart that cleared the road ahead. As deeply rooted as I am in my family and the South,

Mama and Daddy always gave me the freedom to soar and move forward with my life. They always gave me "roots and wings."

My grandmother wasn't as supportive when Mama left her home in South Carolina and moved to Florida, where Daddy was stationed in the Air Force. So, from the time I first got married, Mama told me that she would give me "roots and wings" anytime I moved. The roots of home and family would always be there for me, but my parents wanted me to have the wings of confidence to start my own life and family.

I have two paintings hanging on the wall in my office. One is of the ocean and the beach along the Florida coast, the other of a seagull with outstretched wings. They are reminders of my roots and wings. As Dr. John Trent says in *LifeMapping*, such mementos are "a tangible reminder of the process you've been through. It's a memorial marker that can give you a picture of all you can become."[1] I am deeply grateful to Mama and Daddy for the impact their gift of stability and freedom had on my life. When our children got married, we gave them the gift my parents gave me—roots and wings (and a hammock to start their own family tradition).

Sometimes it's hard to imagine how a simple statement from a parent to a child can ring in his or her mind for years to come. We may not know it at that moment, but the things we say and do influence our children forever—even in their moves.

Moving Is a Really Big Deal

In today's mobile society, job loss, promotions, and transfers are forcing some families to move frequently—across town, across the country, and even around the world. These moves can be difficult for the whole family but particularly for the children. Millions of children and teenagers pack up their belongings and unpack them again in a different home.

Whether they move down the street or three thousand miles away, children need roots to anchor and support them emotionally. They need to know they have an unwavering foundation in the midst of change. Moving is difficult for children because it involves the loss of friends, school, and the familiar things that are a part of their everyday lives. An article in *Parents* magazine stated, "Toddlers will mourn the loss of their room and the house they've always lived in. School-age children will mourn the loss of their friends and the loss of their school. Teenagers, along with mourning all of the above, are likely to feel anger at their parents for a major life change that is beyond their control."[2]

Many times the move is harder for teens than for younger children. For teens, a move comes at a time when they are trying to establish their independence and may be more resistant to change. A move may threaten their identity and self-confidence with their peers.

School-age children want to fit in with friends and activities. Their social styles or skills could make a difference in how quickly they feel like they belong.

A child's age, personality, and temperament will affect how he or she adjusts to the move. Some will adapt easily, never miss a beat, and thrive in their new surroundings. Others might struggle and find it more difficult, and the adjustment could take longer.

Gina, a moving friend with three boys who are nine, twelve, and fourteen, offers this suggestion: "During the first few months, allow for extra one-on-one talk time with each child. Be vulnerable and tell them about the ups and downs of *your* day and how *you* are feeling about the move. They learn to cope with changes as they see how you handle similar situations."

I always say, "Get in the trenches with your children." Let them know that you understand their feelings and concerns because you have some of the same feelings and concerns (age-appropriate). This can be comforting and will help them feel less alone. Speak to them face-to-face, looking into their eyes—kneel down with the little ones; sit down with the older ones.

Here are some additional guidelines to help your children make the transition more smoothly:

- Don't play down the importance of the changes your children are going through. Their world is uprooted too.

- Telling them everything will work out isn't necessarily the best approach. Things don't always turn out as we hope, but we can still trust God's plan.

- Encourage them to express their fears and concerns. If they are too young to verbalize their feelings, help them by asking questions like, "Does moving scare you or make you afraid?"

- Ask your teenagers to tell you what they are feeling. *Listen* and let them do the talking.

- Don't feel that you have to justify or defend the move, or shoulder the blame. You may not be able to solve their moving issues, but you can be understanding.

- Be available to talk, listen, and provide support.

- Introduce change in stages. Don't overwhelm them with everything all at once.

- If your child lashes out in anger, acknowledge his or her feelings. Explain that this is a normal reaction to loss.

- Don't deny your children's feelings; this can increase their sense of isolation.

- Remember, it's normal for them to experience some temporary regression in behavior. Their grades may drop.

- Don't make promises you can't keep.

Intact families or single moms in crisis moves—whether caused by divorce, death of a spouse, job loss, loss of income, or loss of a home—face a critical and often more traumatic transition with their children. Stress can affect both parent and child. Emotions, confusion, insecurity, and anxiety can intensify in these circumstances. You may need to be proactive and seek professional help for your child.

Shelly Miller, in an issue of *Leadership Journal*, recounted her own story of being uprooted by a move. "While transitions are rarely perfect and often full of loss and hardship, we become more hopeful and resilient through adversity. God uses the uncomfortable place of change to shape our identity and prepare us for the future. Having an empathetic, listening heart that engages freely lends courage to our children for the journey no matter what age, situation, or experience."[3]

In addition to the emotional adjustment of moving, children have to deal with two other types of adjustments: social and academic.

Transferring from one school to another can seem overwhelming to children. It "not only tests their academic skills but also forces them to reevaluate who they are and where they fit in the world. The changes in their lives and relationships can lead to feelings of isolation and failure or to feelings of greater competency and higher self-esteem. . . . Most will tell you that the social changes are more frightening, more difficult, and more important."[4]

Jackie, from Delaware, shared this heartwarming story:

> Our move from Iowa to Delaware had been most difficult for our nine-year-old son, Will, who left behind some wonderful buddies with whom he was attached at the hip and the heart. Months after the move, he was still crying almost daily. We were praying for him and with him, coaching him, and generally exhausting our bag of tricks to smooth out his little life.
>
> After Will broke down in tears at school one day, his teacher took him into the hall to try and get to the bottom of his pain. She was aware of the tough time he was having, but, like us, was not seeing much progress. He sobbed about missing Iowa and his friends.
>
> She took him back into the classroom and announced that there would be a change in the social studies curriculum: The third-grade class would study Iowa for a day and hold an Iowa State Fair, with everyone participating. The day was great fun and a huge success for everyone, especially Will.
>
> One of the many issues about moving is that no one

knows you. That day was a turning point. Will's new friends plunged into his world and consequently brought Will into theirs.

I am so grateful to his teacher for being creative and compassionate, willing and able to meet the needs of a broken heart. Her heart simply went out to him and the Holy Spirit filled it in. Sometimes the hands of Jesus touch you in unexpected and profound ways. I was awestruck to stand back and watch God touch my child, not using me, but sending a stranger, now a friend. God moved us, and He moved with us.

According to a study in the journal *American Association for Counseling and Development*, it takes a new student an average of twenty-three days to make friends.[5] Don't panic. It doesn't mean that no one will talk to your child or interact with him or her for twenty-three days. It just means the friend-making process takes time. Perhaps, like Will, your child will have a sensitive and compassionate teacher or leader who will reach out and make a difference in his or her life.

In the meantime, here are some things you can say to children to help them make a smooth transition both academically and socially.

Be patient. It's no fun to feel like an outsider, but eventually you will find your place in your school and community. Caution: Don't be so eager to make friends that you hang out with people who don't have the same values or morals.

Be friendly. Don't wait for others to approach you. To have a friend, you have to be a friend. And don't forget to smile!

Be proactive. Ask a classmate a question about homework or a test. Ask if you can sit with someone during lunch. Ask for help.

Sign up. A great way to meet people who like the same thing as you is to get involved: sports, drama, music, technology, or whatever interests you.

Don't brag. Let others find out how good you are at something by your actions, not your words.

Don't compare. No one wants their school's academics, activities, or sports compared with where you came from.

Take a good look. You learn a lot about a place by observing the people and places around you.

Expect differences. School, culture, food, environment—there may be very little that is similar to where you came from.

Remember your manners. You will be remembered when you are kind, thoughtful, and considerate. Nobody wants to be around someone who is rude, mean, and obnoxious.

I remember sitting in our hotel room during the first two weeks of a hot Phoenix summer. I was on the phone inquiring about any soccer leagues that our children could join. They both loved soccer, and I knew the sooner I could get them involved, the better. We didn't know our way around the city, but with a map, we managed to find the soccer fields. (I didn't have GPS at the time.) As I look back, getting them involved in group activities before school started was a springboard to their adjustment.

We had visited the schools ahead of time to get them acclimated; but, even so, the morning I drove up to the entrance and dropped them off at the door, I saw the apprehension in their eyes. I gave them a big smile and an even bigger hug, and said, "I know you'll have a great first day! Remember, I love you. Now go for it!" I left them in God's hands then, just as I do today. I asked Him to protect, guide, and equip them in their new journeys.

Accentuate the Positive

Remind your children that moving usually turns out to be a positive experience. They will see new places, learn about new cultures, meet new people, and make new friends. They will be learning new things about themselves and discovering strengths they never knew they had. The adventure of change will bring about opportunities, challenges, and great experiences. And most important, the shared experiences of moving can bring your family closer together because you will all need to rely on each other. Just remember: Minimize the negative and accentuate the positive. Your attitude and outlook are contagious!

Heart to Heart

Time for another heart-to-heart, moms! Let's get back to talking about roots and wings for a moment. Yes, it's meaningful to give you all the facts about children moving and suggestions on helping them adjust, but the heart of the matter extends back to something far more significant. You see, what Mama and Daddy gave me went deeper than knowing I had a family and a home that would always be there for me. They gave me a Christ-centered foundation in which my roots could grow deep in the love of Jesus Christ. To be anchored in Christ is the basic security our children need for any transition in life. When they grow up and leave home, children will take with them the knowledge of Christ, which has been deeply rooted within.

Sometimes they may take a different path and go in a different direction, but the Christ-centered foundation that you gave them, or that you are giving them now, will be embedded in their hearts and minds. Never lose heart, never lose hope for your children.

> Train up a child in the way he should go, even when he is old, he will not depart from it.
>
> PROVERBS 22:6

> You shall love the LORD your God with all your heart and with all your soul and with all your might. These words, which I am commanding you today, shall be on your heart. You shall teach them diligently to your sons and shall talk of them when you sit in your house and when you walk by the way and when you lie down and when you rise up.
>
> DEUTERONOMY 6:5-7

> So I have also dedicated him to the LORD; as long as he lives he is dedicated to the LORD.
>
> I SAMUEL 1:28

Pass It On

As you provide the roots in Christ for your children, the next seven steps are vital in their growth.

Principles of faith. Base your values on the Word of God.

> Therefore as you have received Christ Jesus the Lord, so walk in Him, having been firmly rooted and now being built up in Him and established in your faith, just as you were instructed, and overflowing with gratitude.
> COLOSSIANS 2:6-7

Pattern of life. Strive to live a life worthy of imitation that models God's design.

> Therefore be imitators of God, as beloved children.
> EPHESIANS 5:1

Persistence that is immovable. Don't give up. Don't let anything move you from what you believe. Be strong in your faith.

> Be strong in the Lord and in the strength of His might.
> EPHESIANS 6:10

Participation. Feel what your children feel. Laugh when they laugh. Cry when they cry.

> Rejoice with those who rejoice, and weep with those who weep.
> ROMANS 12:15

Praise. Encourage them. Believe in them. Sing to them when they are young. Sing with them when they are grown.

Rejoice in the Lord always; again I will say, rejoice! Let
your gentle spirit be known to all.
PHILIPPIANS 4:4-5

Pray. Let them see you pray, hear you pray, and watch you give God
the credit for the results.

Don't worry about anything; instead, pray about
everything; tell God your needs, and don't forget to
thank him for his answers.
PHILIPPIANS 4:6, TLB

Plan. It's never too late. Plan on giving them roots and wings!

But they that wait upon the Lord shall renew their
strength. They shall mount up with wings like eagles;
they shall run and not be weary; they shall walk and
not faint.
ISAIAH 40:31, TLB

Begin laying the foundation for tomorrow!

Her children rise up and bless her; her husband also,
and he praises her.
PROVERBS 31:28

Unpack Your Survival Box

Twenty-six things to consider for your children after a move:

1. Christen your new home by tying a big bow for each child on
   the front door.
2. When a child cuts his or her bow, take a picture to put in
   your moving-day scrapbook.
3. Print family name and address cards so you and your children
   can give them to new friends. (This makes it easier for new
   friends and neighbors to remember your names.)

4. Encourage them to plant seeds or flowers in the yard. Use this as an illustration for how we all have to put down roots to grow in new soil.

5. Encourage them to invite friends home after school. You provide the pizza.

6. Check out the neighborhood for clues that other children live there. Vans and bikes!

7. Make a family time capsule to open in one year. Include things to do, places to see, and words to describe their feelings now.

8. Establish routine as quickly as possible.

9. Don't do away with all their old toys and familiar possessions. These may give your child a feeling of stability.

10. Have family time to pray together, share feelings, play a game, or read together.

11. Include them in decorating their rooms. Let them choose new bedspreads.

12. Suggest they make posters and decorate them for their bedroom doors.

13. Encourage each one to keep a memory book with pictures and memorabilia of your new city and friends.

14. Walk your younger children to the bus stop in the neighborhood. Strike up a conversation with other parents and children.

15. Suggest they keep a journal to write their thoughts and feelings.

16. Tour the school. Find the restrooms, lunchroom, library. Get involved.

17. Invite moms and kids from the neighborhood, school, or church to come to a get-acquainted party on a Saturday morning. Serve donuts and coffee.

18. Let your kids set up a lemonade stand in your yard or driveway. Kids attract kids!

19. Get them involved in a youth program at church.

20. Write "I love U" or "Have a great day!" on the napkins in their lunchboxes or on a piece of paper tucked in their notebooks.
21. Give them lots of reassurance.
22. Listen, listen, listen. Give them lots of hugs.
23. Pray for them every day.
24. Tuck them in at bedtime.
25. Give them roots in Christ, family, and home.
26. Give them wings of confidence to move forward in their journey of life.

BONUS TIP: A must-have book to help your children transition before, during, and after a move: *But Mom, I Don't Want to Move!* (by yours truly).

I'll get up out of my hammock to welcome you to the next chapter. That's how excited I am to share with you all about making friends after a move!

CHAPTER 14

BORROW AN EGG

*I think if I've learned anything about friendship, it's to hang
in, stay connected, fight for them, and let them fight for
you. Don't walk away, don't be distracted, don't be too busy
or tired, don't take them for granted. Friends are part of the
glue that holds life and faith together. Powerful stuff.*

JON KATZ

HAVE YOU JUST MOVED and feel like you'll never make friends like the
ones you left behind? Or maybe you've lived there a while, and the
right friend hasn't come into your life yet. Do you yearn for someone
you can be yourself with? Someone who'll accept you without makeup
and in your grubbiest clothes? Who won't judge your messy house or
your messy life?

You are not alone.

For years, my porch and my hammock have been my resting place,
my place of solitude where I steal away for quiet moments and find
soothing comfort. My porch is a setting where new friendships are
formed and old ones enriched through soul-searching conversations
and sharing.

My hammock is a safe place for an uprooted friend to share her
heart. Many tears of loss and grief have been shed there. I can think
of no better place for you and me to talk about friendship than sitting

on my porch. So come. Join me as you read Chris's story and the rest of this chapter. Imagine you are gently swinging back and forth in my hammock as I sit across from you in my rocking chair.

"We used to talk on the phone every day," Chris shared with me as she relaxed in the hammock. "Beth was closer to me than a sister. She was so much a part of my life. We understood each other's feelings and thoughts; we knew what the other was going to say even before she said it. There wasn't anything we wouldn't do for one another." With her feet, Chris stopped the hammock from swinging, looked across at me, and said, "No one can ever take her place. I miss her terribly!"

The separation from Beth, her dearest friend, was devastating to Chris. I knew this wasn't the time for platitudes or shallow words, telling her she would find another close friend in time. For the moment, just the gentle sway of the hammock and my presence was enough.

Chris spent the afternoon with me on the porch. We talked a lot about friendship, what a gift a close friend is to us, and how many people go through life without ever experiencing a deep, meaningful friendship. As Chris got up from the hammock, she remarked, "I look back and cherish the memories Beth and I made together. I think I'll write her a letter, telling her what a difference she has made in my life."

Chris and Beth's friendship remains close today, and they have adjusted to the distance between them. No one has taken Beth's place as a cherished friend, but Chris has started to meet new people and make new friends. It's a joy to watch her friendships grow.

When we move, so many of the things we leave behind can be replaced rather quickly, and life then resumes its pace with a fairly normal rhythm. Friendships are the exception. *The void created by the absence of a dear friend leaves a gaping wound in our hearts, and the longing for shared intimacy keeps us out of step with the world around us.*

What a Difference a Friend Makes

What is it that makes a friend a friend? Why is it that one person entwines her life and heart with ours, making "parting such sweet sorrow"?

Dee Brestin says it beautifully in her book *The Friendships of Women*. "When I talk to my closest female friends, I feel my soul being sunned and watered when they ask questions, drawing out the deep waters of my soul, and as well when they empathize, rejoicing when I rejoice, weeping when I weep."[1]

Let me tell you about some friends who have knitted their lives with mine. Remember my friend Nancy from Atlanta? When we moved, I couldn't find anyone to take her place. But God did the most incredible thing; He gave me another Nancy in Phoenix! She is a friend and sister in Christ who is precious and dear to my heart. How blessed I am to have *two* Nancys—one in the South and one in the West! Over the years, they have taught me about unconditional love between friends. The love they pour over my family and me has been immeasurable.

Then God just kept multiplying wonderful godly women in my life, far beyond all I could ever imagine. These are women who sometimes walk ahead of me and lead the way, sometimes walk behind me and follow, but always walk with me, holding my hand.

Together, we have celebrated life, shared in joy and sorrow, laughter and tears, illness and death. We have stood by each other in marriage and divorce, the good times and the tough times. They have accepted me just as I am, encouraged me, held me accountable for my actions, affirmed my good qualities, and helped me change my bad ones. They have been sensitive to my needs, served me unabashedly, and prayed for me faithfully.

Our lives are a far cry from being perfect. Thank the Lord, we are over that "do more, be more, have more" mentality. Our imperfections draw us near to each other and to Jesus.

First and foremost, the foundation of our friendship is built on our common bond in Christ. We do not measure our love and devotion to one another by the world's standard of who we are, how much we have, or what we wear. Our standard is based on a Christ-centered love. We are all equal in His eyes. Our love and devotion to each other is the same love and devotion that Christ has for us. Because we have received His love, we can then give that love to each other.

There are many endearing stories of friendship recounted in the Bible, but four, in particular, I want to share with you. Notice how each person either moved or traveled from one place to another—to escape circumstances, to be with family, to start over, or to serve in ministry. It's another reminder to us that throughout the Bible, we read about God's people moving to or from something or someone.

Jonathan and David (1 Samuel 18:1-4). Jonathan was the closest friend David ever had. They based their friendship on their mutual commitment to God, not just to each other. They let nothing come between them—neither family issues nor career. They drew closer together when their friendship was tested. Jonathan's father, Saul, was trying to kill David, which forced him into hiding. Despite life-threatening circumstances, Jonathan and David remained friends to the end. *Loyal* friends.

Elizabeth and Mary (Luke 1:5-80). Elizabeth, a deeply spiritual woman, became pregnant later in life and was the mother of John the Baptist. As you know, Mary became pregnant at a young age and was the mother of Jesus. Mary traveled from Nazareth to the hill country of Judea to visit her relative, Elizabeth. Both pregnant, they immediately bonded through the unique gifts God had given them. Mary stayed with Elizabeth for three months and Elizabeth became Mary's mentor. They were faithful to each other and to God. *Faithful* friends.

Ruth and Naomi (the book of Ruth). Naomi traveled from Bethlehem to Moab and later returned to Bethlehem with Ruth. As daughter-in-law (Ruth) and mother-in-law (Naomi), their greatest bond was their faith in God and a strong mutual commitment to each other, despite their differences. Each of them tried to do what was best for the other. *Committed* friends.

Paul and Timothy (Philippians 2:19-22 and 1 and 2 Timothy). They went on missionary journeys together. Their relationship began as teacher and pupil, but they developed into close friends and coworkers. Timothy probably knew Paul better than anyone and became like a son to him. *Devoted* friends.

Jesus—Our Role Model

The best way to learn about a Christian friendship is to go back to the source—Jesus Christ. He is the one who imparts love, the one who models love.

Jesus' actions and words changed the landscape of what relationships look like. (Read Matthew, Mark, Luke, and John to learn all about the life of Jesus.)

He demonstrated what it looks like to have an "observable love" for others. Jesus came to live among us so He could relate to us and we could relate to Him. He has walked in our shoes. He has felt our pain and joy, our acceptance and rejection, our disappointment and despair.

Jesus' twelve disciples were His close friends. I'm sure they laughed together, argued together, and knew each other's strengths and weaknesses. For three years—day and night—the disciples watched the expressions on Jesus' face, caught the tone of His voice, experienced His firm but loving correction, witnessed the pain of His crucifixion, and experienced the power of His resurrection.

Within the twelve, a smaller group—Peter, James, and John—knew Jesus more personally. To those three He revealed the fullness of His glory and the depths of His suffering.

Among the three, John was His intimate friend, the one He called His beloved disciple. James was deeply committed to Jesus and the first disciple to be martyred. Peter recognized Jesus as the Messiah, denied Christ, but repented. All three were with Jesus at His transfiguration.

There were also close friends outside the twelve disciples who shared His inner circle—Lazarus, Mary, and Martha. Jesus taught them all about His love, but they *experienced* it through their friendship with Him. If we observe the kind of relationship Jesus had with His disciples, then the foundation for a Christian friendship becomes so clear.

- He shared His life with them.
- He spent time with them.

- He prayed with them.
- He was committed to them.
- He built trust with them.
- He accepted them.
- He encouraged them.
- He listened to them.
- He forgave them.

If you ever played the game follow the leader as a child, then you'll get the hang of what to do very quickly. You do what the leader does. Just that simple. I can remember running around outside in the yard imitating whatever our leader did—from waving my arms, to skipping, to singing. It's not just a game now; following my Leader is a way of life. Don't complicate following Jesus. Just do what He did, and still does, in our lives today.

Do you get it? He didn't just teach the disciples about love; He expressed it to them in a way they could see, touch, and feel. His love was tangible. In other words, He didn't just talk the talk; He walked the walk. He was a powerful role model for what a godly relationship looks like.

> A new commandment I give to you, that you love one
> another, even as I have loved you, that you also love one
> another. By this all men will know that you are My disciples,
> if you have love for one another.
> JOHN 13:34-35

Kathy Narramore expresses it well in her book on friendship, *Kindred Spirits*:

> It is as if Jesus were saying to each of us, "You will experience
> my love as you love each other. You can know about my love
> from my Word but you are to experience it through your
> friendships. This will be possible not only because I will be

with you, but because I will be in you, through my Spirit empowering you." It seems God planned for us to do our spiritual and emotional maturing in relationships with others. Growth takes place in the context of relationships. Christian friendships are designed to promote our growth toward maturity by helping us see God and ourselves. They can also help meet our deep emotional needs as we accept, care for, encourage, forgive, and are committed to one another. As we do this for one another, we reflect the Lord to one another.[2]

Look for This Kind of Friend

Have you ever looked and looked for something only to find that it was right there all along, right under your nose? You look in books, blogs, magazines, on TV, social media, the web, even YouTube—anything to know where and how to find a friend. And yet you're looking in all the wrong places. The friend you're looking for has been there all along. You were so busy, you missed feeling His presence. You were so desperate to find a friend, you overlooked the best Friend of all.

Jesus is your go-to friend, no doubt about it. You can always lean on Him, and He'll always be there to catch you. *No matter where you move, He's gone before you, He's got your back, and He walks beside you.* He will be there when you need Him to listen to your heart, to fill the emptiness, and to comfort you. Embrace Him as a friend *first*. In His perfect timing, He will bring new friends to fill your life.

When you follow Jesus as your Leader, and as a way of life, you will want to look for a friend:

- who is an extension of Jesus Christ, not a substitute for Him.
- who will love you unconditionally and accept you as you are, as she points you toward Jesus.
- who will walk with you through thick and thin, as she reminds you that Jesus cares and understands.
- who will pray with you and for you.

- who will teach you about Jesus through how she lives her life and the choices she makes.
- who carries a triple-A card, like Jesus did! Jesus was Available, Accessible, and Authentic. Look for someone who is all three.

This is an example of the friendship that Joan and Margie have had over the years. When they met, they were both newcomers and had moving in common. Joan spoke freely about Jesus. She lived an observable love for Margie. She bought her a Bible, prayed with her, walked with her through hard times, and accepted her unconditionally. Margie began to grow in her faith. She learned what it meant to have a personal relationship with Jesus. Today she is a strong believer and follows Jesus as a way of life.

I love the way Jerry and Mary White describe a friend in their book *Friends & Friendship*: "A friend is a trusted confidant to whom I am mutually drawn as a companion and an ally, whose love for me is not dependent on my performance, and whose influence draws me closer to God."[3]

Friendships on the Move

Were you a little bit curious about my chapter title, "Borrow an Egg"? Well, you see, it all boils down to how to make new friends! When any of my friends move, I give them a special little going-away present. In a small pink gift bag with pink tissue paper, I include a small bird's nest with tiny eggs (from a craft store), an egg (the plastic or wooden ones that are usually on sale after Easter), a bookmark I create that says, "Bloom Wherever You're Planted," a small mirror, and a six-inch piece of white rope with a pink ribbon tied around it. (Sounds like a lot, but I keep several of each on hand.)

As I give the gift bag to them I say, "The first thing you must do when you move is to make your nest a home. Weave it with the fruit of the Spirit. Second, borrow an egg from a neighbor (or anything else you might need). It's all about getting a conversation started. This is the easiest way to meet your neighbor and start a friendship. Third, put this bookmark in your Bible as a reminder to find a church. After that, you must look in this mirror as a reminder that it all begins with you. Finally, hold on tight to this rope. It's a reminder of God's love, His Word, and His promises woven into your life."

Many of my friends have written that they still have these little reminders and have followed these simple steps to help them adjust. Can you pretend that I just gave that same going-away gift to you? Let it be a reminder that I care about you as you move, just as I do about my other moving friends.

Here are some other ways to stay in touch over the miles with a friend who has moved:

- Send a plant or flowers to arrive on the day she is moving into her new home. Write on the card, "Bloom Wherever You're Planted!"
- Make the first move. . . . Send encouraging one-line texts, such as: "You can do this!" or "I thank God for every remembrance of you."
- Use your phone, e-mail, or social media to send a picture of you holding a hand-written sign that says, "I miss you already!" "Happy birthday!" or other encouragement.
- It's worth repeating that one of my favorite ways to stay in touch is to send a "party in a card" to celebrate a birthday. Include a deflated balloon, confetti, a birthday napkin, a birthday streamer, and anything else that can fit in an envelope.
- Make advance plans to visit each other or get together somewhere for a girls' getaway weekend.
- E-mail round-robin letters to several friends to stay in touch with what's going on in each other's lives.
- In an e-mail, attach a link to an article or blog that reminds you of your friend. Send a note with it that says, "This reminded me of you" or "I thought of you when I read this."
- Occasionally send a small gift as a token of remembrance and friendship. It means a lot to receive a package from a long-distance friend. It could be as simple as a small devotional book.

Heart to Heart

In addition to my love for flowers, birds, and hammocks, I love the beach. I've collected seashells from the beach for many years. Come with me, and we will stroll the shoreline and look for seashells as we have our heart-to-heart talk.

Seashells are a lot like friends. No two are exactly alike; each is one of a kind. I love adding new shells, as well as new friends, to those I already have. I find shells scattered along the beach. I find friends along the shores of life. Sometimes it takes a lot of time and effort to find special shells and special friends. I always take the shells and the friends with me everywhere I go. Each has lasting value to me, and I treasure the memories of where and how I found them. May your life be enriched and blessed by the friends you find along life's shoreline as you move.

 ## Unpack Your Survival Box

Twenty-five ways to find and make new friends:

1. Be approachable.
2. Take the opportunities God gives you. When someone invites you to do something this week, invite her to do something next week.
3. Find a church.
4. Strike up a conversation with another shopper in the grocery store. (She might be your neighbor.)
5. Be proactive; make the first move.
6. Ask someone to be your prayer partner.
7. Go to a neighborhood garage sale.
8. When you are invited to do things, say yes even if you feel shy, may not know how to get around town, or won't know anyone there.
9. Offer to carpool.
10. Send a card or a note to someone who needs to be encouraged.

11. Be available.
12. Invite someone to lunch.
13. Join a women's Bible study.
14. Pray for God to send just the right person to be your friend.
15. Find a need in your church or community and fill it.
16. Walk your children to the bus stop and talk to other mothers.
17. Go for a walk or a hike and greet everyone along the way.
18. Be yourself.
19. Be a good listener.
20. Put on a happy face and smile—be friendly, warm, and genuine.
21. Find something you have in common with people you meet.
22. Ask questions.
23. Volunteer. Volunteer. Volunteer.
24. Find a class you want to take, a club you want to join, a cause you want to support, or a committee you want to serve on.
25. Remember, to have a friend, you must be a friend!

Sometimes, to make friends, all you need to do is show up. As C. S. Lewis said, "Friendship is born at that moment when one [person] says to another, 'What! You too? I thought that no one but myself . . .'"

PART 3

Move Forward

As you and I walked together through the process of starting over in part 2, I trust you began to feel renewed hope for yourself, a new perspective on creating a home, new insight into strengthening your marriage, and a better understanding of how to help your children. It is my prayer that you have made the choice to allow God to mold you through this process, and that you will continue to grow deep roots in Him. If you've begun to do that during this transition, you truly are on the road to a new beginning. Now you are ready to begin the last process and move forward.

As I made the choice to go forward, I came to know my God more intimately as He moved with me through all the changes of life. It was time to come full circle by finding contentment and peace in the midst of my circumstances, by making choices for a more balanced life, and by starting to reach out to others around me. I realized that there comes a time when I have to take God's biblical principles and begin to live them out in my words and actions.

Because I had allowed God to *mend* and *mold* me, He could then *mature* me in my walk with Him. I invite you to join me and move forward as we continue our unpacking journey in these chapters. This section is the ribbon that ties the book together.

To let go allows God to mend you.

To start over allows God to mold you.

To move forward allows God to mature you.

CHAPTER 15

COME FULL CIRCLE AFTER A MOVE

The faithful love of the LORD never ends! His mercies never cease. Great is his faithfulness; his mercies begin afresh each morning.

LAMENTATIONS 3:22-23, NLT

BEFORE YOU GO ANY FURTHER, I want you to stop and give yourself a big *hug* from me! I love cheering you on every step of the way. You probably don't realize how close you really are to coming full circle and moving forward with your life by choosing to let go and start over. It must be like a breath of fresh air to realize that by processing those two stages, you are going to be all right!

Just between the two of us—I believe in you. I have confidence in who you are. I'm convinced you are going to make it. You've already come this far. I'm certain you're a different person from the inside out. You've taken the time to examine your life, to address your heart, and to get a new perspective on your move.

A Matter of Choice

I want you to have a better understanding of how to *live above your circumstances, live in contentment and peace,* and *live with joy* as you choose to press on and move forward.

Each of these comes from within you and will have a profound impact on your life when you go through a move or any life change.

Check out the stories of Lisa, Claire, and Patty to get a good picture of what I'm talking about.

Lisa's husband had a difficult time finding work during the economic downturn, so they had to move four times in seven years of marriage. She faced one crisis after another during those seven years: breast cancer, a new baby, marriage issues, and one move after another. A neighbor asked Lisa to join a Moving On After Moving In study in their neighborhood for women who had moved. Lisa got involved and never missed the study. She embraced the principles of choosing to let go, start over, and move forward. Lisa began to focus on God instead of her circumstances. She began to study the Bible and memorize scripture passages with the other women. She and her husband started going to counseling. Slowly, over time, emotional healing began. Lisa came full circle in her process of moving as she learned to trust God and live above her circumstances.

Next, let's look at Claire. This was her eighth move as a corporate expat wife. This move, however, was different from the others. Though the transition from Hong Kong back to the States was difficult, Claire felt more peaceful and less anxious than she had in the past. She knew the peace didn't come from her circumstances but from the time she spent in prayer each day. International relocations always seemed glamorous to her family and friends, but in reality, they were a strain on her marriage. Claire and her husband had begun to drift apart. Through a men's accountability group, her husband became more aware of what a woman goes through emotionally with the constant upheaval of being relocated. He realized that a move isn't just something you do; it's something you feel. He became more understanding and supportive. Their marriage relationship grew stronger, and they became closer than they had been in a long time. Claire experienced a contentment she had never known before.

Patty, a widow from the boomer generation, had to work to make ends meet. While her friends were thinking about retirement, she was looking for a job. When she went to work for an insurance company, she knew a transfer to a branch office across the city was inevitable. Patty was excited about moving. She was ready for a change and new surroundings. She understood how important it was to begin to move forward after loss and a life change. As a woman of great faith and maturity, Patty lives with a joy that isn't dependent on her circumstances.

What do these three women have in common? They have made a choice to keep God as the focus in their lives, not the circumstances around them. Their focus is vertical, not horizontal. They have learned to *respond to God first, instead of responding to people and situations.*

In *The Beauty of Beholding God,* Darien Cooper says, "Marriage, career, children, social status, possessions, and even friends do not satisfy the inner void in our lives. They are meant to be enjoyed, but none are life-giving."[1]

Only a relationship with Jesus Christ can fill the void in your life. Jesus says, "I am the way, and the truth, and the life" (John 14:6).

Refocus. Redirect. Refill.

I know you're thinking, *How do I live above, and not under, my circumstances? How do I live in contentment and peace, and live with joy—after a hard move or any major life change?*

When you make the choice to live above your circumstances by changing the focus of your life, then living in contentment and peace, and living with joy, can come.

You see, my friend,

> when you focus on God by knowing His character and His
> attributes,
> when you saturate your mind and heart with His Word,
> when you begin to grasp the magnitude of His love and care
> for you,
> when you allow Him to use your struggles to transform you,
> when you embrace His presence with your whole being,

when you finally recognize that life is more than your circumstances
and you really "get" Jesus,
then you will know the contentment, peace, and joy that come
from an intimate relationship with Him.

Did you ever think that maybe, just maybe, God could be using
your circumstances to draw you closer to Him? You may not have recognized emptiness as a thirst for Him that only He can fill.

Focus on Who God Is

As you choose to redirect your focus to God, look at some of His
attributes and the very nature of His character. They define who He
is. This will begin to quench that thirst.

- God is *sovereign*. (He is in total control of everything.) "For
  God is the King of all the earth" (Psalm 47:7).
- God is *righteous*. (He is always good and whatever He does is
  always right.) "The LORD is righteous in all His ways and kind
  in all His deeds" (Psalm 145:17).
- God is *just*. (He is fair in all of His actions.) "All His ways are
  just; a God of faithfulness and without injustice, righteous and
  upright is He" (Deuteronomy 32:4).
- God is *unchangeable*. (He is always the same in His nature, His
  character, and His will.) "In ages past you laid the foundations
  of the earth and made the heavens with your hands! They shall
  perish, but you go on forever" (Psalm 102:25-26, TLB).
- God is *loving*. (He loves us beyond measure, so much that He
  sent Christ to die for us.) "But God demonstrates His own love
  toward us, in that while we were yet sinners, Christ died for us"
  (Romans 5:8).
- God is *eternal*. (He has no beginning and no end.) "Now to the
  King eternal, immortal, invisible, the only God, be honor and
  glory forever and ever. Amen" (1 Timothy 1:17).
- God is *everywhere*. (His presence is with us wherever we are.)

"The eyes of the LORD are in every place, watching the evil and the good" (Proverbs 15:3).

- God is *all knowing.* (He knows everything, all the time.) "O LORD, You have searched me and known me" (Psalm 139:1).
- God is *all powerful.* (He is strong and mighty.) "I am the Lord, the God of all mankind; is there anything too hard for me?" (Jeremiah 32:27, TLB)
- God is *truthful.* (He is honest and faithful.) "In the hope of eternal life, which God, who cannot lie, promised long ages ago" (Titus 1:2).

The key to your peace, security, and stability when your world is uprooted is to rest and rely on God's character. *When you keep your focus on God, you can come out on the other side of your circumstances in victory, not as a victim.*

Focus on His Word

I know I've said it before, but "run, don't walk" to Scripture. We need it for the very fiber of our souls. It meets us right smack in the middle of any situation, anytime, under any circumstance. Yes, there will be days when Scripture won't feel new and fresh. I've had those times when I seemed to walk right over the words. But I keep going back to the chapter and verse until it begins to penetrate my heart and mind. Then I find myself running to His Word to be filled with:

- Permanent security
- Soothing comfort
- Calming peace
- Clear guidance
- Enduring hope
- Positive encouragement
- Timeless truth

(You can probably come up with even more discoveries of your own.)

I suggest you try reading Scripture aloud. You not only see the Word; you hear and say the Word. Pray Scripture passages by inserting your own name or the name of someone you're praying for. With the help of a concordance, Bible dictionary, or reference book, do a word or phrase study to understand what a particular word or phrase means. This will help you understand a verse or chapter more clearly. Get to know the people in the Bible by researching a favorite person or story. Choose a topical word like *joy*, *hope*, or *peace* and use a concordance to look up the Scripture passages that use that word. Write the word at the top of a page in a blank journal and, beneath it, list the Scripture verses you find most meaningful.

Make sure you unpack your Bible first after you move. You don't want to skip a beat by being distracted with all the things on your to-do list. Redirect your focus to God and His Word.

The Big Picture

This much I know—God doesn't always change your situation, but He will give you strength, hope, and encouragement so you can face your circumstances and keep on going. You can take that to the bank and cash it, friends. The things I learned going through the valleys in life taught me more about God and His faithfulness than I could have ever learned on the mountaintops.

> So we do not look at what we can see right now, the troubles
> all around us, but we look forward to the joys in heaven
> which we have not yet seen. The troubles will soon be over,
> but the joys to come will last forever.
> 2 CORINTHIANS 4:18, TLB

Maybe you didn't want to move and leave your family and friends.
Maybe you're terribly lonely.
Maybe your marriage is suffering from the transition.
Maybe your children are rebelling over having to move.
Maybe you're financially strapped with two house payments.
Maybe life just stinks right now with all the losses you've experienced.

Regardless of your circumstances, cling to God's faithfulness.

Trust Him for what you don't know, don't understand, or can't see. Difficult or devastating circumstances can hit you hard, knock you off your feet, and leave you breathless.

Pull yourself up by your bootstraps, girl.

Dust off your dancing shoes; you can do it.

Lace up those walking shoes; you can make it.

Put those stilettos back on and stand up straight.

Face the day head-on, knowing you walk in God's strength and in His grace and mercy.

The issues, problems, and trials in your life will constantly change. God never changes. He is our anchor in the storm. He is our lighthouse to guide us when we cannot see what lies ahead.

Jesus Christ is the same yesterday and today and forever.

HEBREWS 13:8

Give all your worries to Him because He cares for you.

1 PETER 5:7, NLV

My friend Mary often says when any of us are in crisis, "Do you walk by faith or by sight?" It sure brings us back to center very quickly. Yes, I'll walk by faith any day! I know God sees the big picture of my life. I don't need to know everything from beginning to end, because God already does. Through faith in Him, I can encounter life's problems with confidence, knowing that He will see me through. My God is bigger than whatever circumstances may surround me!

Trust in the LORD forever, for in God the LORD, we have an everlasting Rock.

ISAIAH 26:4

For we walk by faith, not by sight.

2 CORINTHIANS 5:7

Heart to Heart

Let's take a break and have a good heart-to-heart talk. I've been encouraging you to look beyond your circumstances. Let me paint a picture for you. Pretend you're standing on a shore, looking across the water to the opposite shore where there is solid ground. Imagine your circumstances are stormy waters in between the two shores, and God is your safe and solid ground on the other side. He'll do everything possible to bring you across that water to Him. He'll give you the lifeline of hope, He'll give you a sunny day in the midst of your rough waters, and He'll give you strength to keep paddling toward the shore—to Him.

Sometimes you might get distracted by other things in the water and go off course. Just remember to keep your eyes focused on Him. Don't let the current or the undertow pull you under the water. Keep paddling. Once you reach the other side and look back, you'll see your circumstances a lot more clearly and be better equipped to handle another storm if it comes your way. The best part about getting through any storm is that you want to fall in the arms of Jesus with gratitude.

> As they were sailing along . . . a fierce gale of wind descended
> on the lake, and they began to be swamped and to be in
> danger. "Master, Master, we are perishing!" And He got
> up and rebuked the wind and the surging waves, and they
> stopped, and it became calm. And He said to them, "Where
> is your faith?"
>
> LUKE 8:23-25

A Desert Experience

How many times have you said, "It sure would make this move a lot easier, if only—"? One of my moving friends, Dianna, put it best when she said, "'If only' is a delusion. It's being discontent with what God has provided."

Dianna's insight reminds me of our Old Testament friends, the Israelites, from the Camp of Complaining. They wandered through the wilderness discontented and grumbling. Initially they wanted to leave

Egypt to go to the Promised Land for a better life. But the people soon became dissatisfied and complained bitterly about their trek through the wilderness. They didn't like the water. They didn't like the food. They didn't listen to God. "Oh, that we were back in Egypt," they moaned (Exodus 16:3, TLB). They had a bad case of "if only," "what if," and the "have-nots."

How many of you have had a dry period of discontentment—a desert experience—after you settled in? That's a pretty normal part of the moving process for most of us.

After the dust settles, reality hits. That's when it's easy to look around and compare, or think "if only" or focus on the "have-nots." The dust does settle and the desert experiences do come. Expect them and don't be so hard on yourself. You're not always going to be happy. You're not always going to like where you live, and you're not always going to have everything come together like you expected. And you're certainly not always going to feel spiritual! You are a woman in process, not a woman who is a perfect, finished product. Just promise me that you won't be like the Israelites! Listen to God and trust Him to lead you around obstacles. Don't get stuck in the valley of discontentment.

Do You Want It, or Do You Need It?

One of the best definitions of *contentment* is found in Philippians 4:11-12: "Not that I was ever in need, for I have learned how to get along happily whether I have much or little. I know how to live on almost nothing or with everything. I have learned the secret of contentment in every situation, whether it be a full stomach or hunger, plenty or want" (TLB).

Read the passage again. Do you know the secret to Paul's contentment? It's being satisfied with what God has or has not given him. I know that not all moves are up the ladder. Some are down the ladder, as a result of job losses and company cutbacks. You might have had to adjust to a lower income, a smaller home, and fewer possessions. Can you say, "It is well with my soul," in spite of your circumstances? Is Jesus enough when everything is taken away?

Bill and I experienced downsizing in one of our many moves. At the time, we were in a financial crunch and had to make some major lifestyle changes. We discovered, like Paul, that "my God will supply all your needs according to His riches in glory in Christ Jesus" (Philippians 4:19). One of the things Bill would say to me many times when I would be having my own pity party over wanting this or that was, "God may not supply all our wants, but He sure has supplied all our needs, Susan." Lesson learned.

How do you learn contentment? Look closely at what Paul says in Philippians 4:11-12: "I have *learned* how to get along happily. . . . I have *learned* the secret of contentment." He uses the word *learned* in the past tense. Paul had a history, a track record, with the faithfulness of God. God had met Paul's needs in the past, and Paul had faith that God would meet them in the future. The secret was drawing on God's power and relying on God's promises for strength to be content. With contentment comes peace—a peace that is beyond all understanding to those who don't know Jesus. "He will keep in perfect peace all those who trust in him, whose thoughts turn often to the Lord!" (Isaiah 26:3, TLB).

In addition to what Paul teaches us, here are some things you can do to help you live in contentment: abide, be grateful, and choose joy.

Abide (to dwell; to live or reside in a place). You don't have to follow a formula to spend time with Jesus. So many times people get so focused on the process of studying the Bible, they lose sight of the person of Jesus. Simply abide. Abide in God's Word; read the Bible like it was written to you personally—because it was. Abide in prayer; talk to God like He's there with you—because He is. Abide in His promises; believe and trust His Word—because He keeps a promise. Just abide in Him. I suggest you zero in on John 15:1-10 for a clear picture of what it means to abide in Jesus. He is the vine. You are the branch. Stay connected, and from Him will flow everything you need. In fact, go ahead and read the whole book of John. It's all about our awesome Jesus. It's pretty amazing.

Be grateful. A grateful heart brings you back to Jesus. Luke 17:11-17 tells us that only one of the ten lepers who were healed went back to thank Jesus. Being grateful for what you have not only brings contentment but teaches you a lot about God's grace. He has shown His unmerited favor to all of us in some way or another. Whether you have much or little, it is sufficient. Don't miss the moment of thanking Him daily for His grace in your life.

Choose joy. First of all, let me share a little insight I've learned through the years on the difference between joy and happiness.

- Joy comes from inside you, deep within your heart.
- Joy is the manifestation of the contentment and peace you feel in your soul.
- Joy is an outward expression of an unshakable inner relationship with God.
- Joy is not determined by the external; it's all about the internal.
- You can be joyful regardless of your situation or circumstances.

Joy surpasses happiness and keeps on going deep within—so deep that it permeates your whole demeanor. Joy is evident in your eyes, your smile, your words, and even the way you walk. (Be mindful of things that rob you of joy—fear, worry, and things!)

Happiness, on the other hand, is a result of what happens around you, to you, or for you.

If everything is going great and according to plan, then naturally you're going to be happy. Of course you can also feel joy and happiness at the same time, but they are coming from two different sources.

But let me set something straight right now—I don't always feel joyful *or* happy. I'm not some perfect Pollyanna by any means. There are days that I struggle, nights that are sleepless, and times when I can't seem to pull my life together. *I don't claim the joy in me; I claim the Holy Spirit in me.* Like His Word says, "I have told you this so that you will be filled with my joy. Yes, your cup of joy will overflow!" (John 15:11, TLB).

I choose to trust Him when I don't have all the answers, rest in Him when I'm in turmoil, and rely on Him when I don't understand.

It's like Tim Hansel says in his book *You Gotta Keep Dancin'*, "Joy . . . occurs in spite of difficult situations. . . . It is not a feeling; it is a *choice*. It is not based upon circumstances; it is based upon attitude."[2] He quotes Paul Sailhamer, who said, "Joy is that deep settled confidence that God is in control of every area of my life."[3]

Tribute to a Smile

When I think of someone who chose joy in her life, I remember a former newcomer, Vicki. One of the special qualities about Vicki was her beautiful smile. When she moved here, she was married and had a young daughter. Then her husband left her. Every time I saw Vicki at church with her daughter, she was smiling. She had chosen to be joyful in spite of her circumstances. It was obvious that her smile was not forced or faked and that her joy was an expression of God's presence in her life.

Then Vicki was diagnosed with cancer. Even then, every time I saw her, she had that radiant smile woven with joy and peace on her face. The last time I talked with Vicki she was bedridden at home. Cancer had slowly taken over her body, but it hadn't taken her smile, her joy, or her unshakable faith in God. Vicki taught me about real joy. I will always be grateful that our paths crossed, and that I had the privilege of catching a closer glimpse of Jesus through her joy.

 ## Unpack Your Survival Box

Five Ways to Live Above Your Circumstances:
- Make the choice
- Change your focus
- Persevere
- Be intentional
- Don't give up

Five Ways to Live in Contentment and Peace:
- Abide in Jesus
- Saturate yourself in His Word
- Trust Him
- Slow down
- Be grateful

Five Ways to Live with Joy:
- Jesus in you
- Claim it
- Confidence in Christ
- Release fear and worry
- Count your blessings

Congratulations! You are in the process of coming full circle and getting ready to move forward. In the next chapter you're going to be equipped to move in a new direction.

CHAPTER 16

BACK IN THE SADDLE AGAIN!

*In everything you do, put God first, and he will direct you
and crown your efforts with success.*
PROVERBS 3:6, TLB

WHEN I REACH FOR lettuce in my grocery store's produce section, I'm always attracted to the cut-up, prepackaged variety of lettuce sold in bags. I will admit, it's a convenient way to make a quick salad when you're on the go.

But when I shop for lettuce, I always pick up each head, or bunch, and examine it closely to get the freshest one possible. So instead of the prepackaged salad, I normally defer to buying good old-fashioned lettuce-in-the-raw, as I call it, because I'm a creature of habit. I'm often reluctant to change my lettuce routine.

Are you a creature of habit too? Do you find it hard to change old ways? Some habits are worth keeping, but others might need some cleaning out.

You might want to think about what aspects of your life need a good change. They may be important matters of the heart or just minor things in the course of a day that need rethinking or revising since you've moved.

Now is the time to "turn over a new leaf" (as in lettuce—get it?)! What a great time to make some changes that will give you new direction and make your life easier and more enjoyable.

What's It Going to Take?

It's hard for me to pass up a scrumptious muffin. It's just as hard for me to go on a diet to lose a few pounds because I can't find a diet that says, "You are allowed one scrumptious, oversize, fattening, but healthy muffin a day." Since this type of muffin doesn't exist, I've just decided to collect diets instead of going on them and to choose, instead, a lifestyle of healthy eating. But it's not easy. In all honesty, every now and then I do splurge on a scrumptious muffin—or half of one—as a treat.

All this muffin talk is just to say, I struggle with self-discipline in some areas of my life, as most of you probably do. I take many detours just walking from my bedroom to the kitchen to get a cup of coffee. When I sit down at my desk to file (I'm a piler, not a filer), I find numerous reasons to get back up. I can also easily be distracted from a task because people will always be more important to me than a to-do list. Can you identify with me? Still, I know there are times I need to discipline myself to get the important things done.

Self-discipline is a springboard to help me get my life in order—and it will also help you get your life in order (whatever order looks like for you) after you settle in. You might want to start over and make some new goals, do a little reprioritizing, some reorganizing, maybe even some minimizing. In Earl Wilson's book *Self-Discipline*, he states, "Self-discipline is nothing more than a series of small choices which protect the minutes of your life, allowing you to become a more productive person."[1]

But there are different kinds of productivity. Actively productive involves doing: having something to "show" for your time. Quietly productive is taking time to be; it's an inner work, unseen to others (and, possibly, even to yourself), but just as important.

Sometimes I don't want to be actively productive, but quietly productive. Though it can be hard for me to do, I have learned to pull away from my busy life and sit. Sit and read, sit and listen, sit and pray, sit and count my blessings, sit and think. But even sitting requires discipline.

The benefit of taking the time to be still, quiet, and reflective restores and refreshes me. It is during those quiet times that I feel centered on what's most important—my relationship with Christ. It's when I can become calm and settled in my spirit. It's when I take a deep breath, recharge, and refill for my busy life.

On the other hand, I have a friend who is actively productive as the mother of four children and a nurse working the night shift. She gets home from work in the morning in time to fix breakfast and get her children off to school. Before she goes to work at night, she prepares dinner, gets the kids ready for school the next day, and puts them to bed. It requires a lot of self-discipline to manage a schedule like that, but she is committed to making it work, and it certainly helps to make her family's life run more smoothly.

Wise Words

When I got married and entered the next season of life, my daddy gave me wise counsel. "In the Bible you can find everything you need to know about how to live your life. That's the best life instruction book and how-to manual you can ever have." He was right. I've found instruction for behavior, relationships, finances, raising children, and being a wife, mother, and friend. To this day, I continue to get clear direction, for even the smallest things, right within its pages. I even find instruction for self-discipline and goal setting.

Philippians 3:13-14 provides biblical insights and wise words regarding self-discipline: "One thing I do: forgetting what lies behind and reaching forward to what lies ahead, I press on toward the goal for the prize of the upward call of God in Christ Jesus."

Do you see the *four key phrases* in these verses which are necessary for self-discipline? They are: *one thing, forgetting, reaching forward,* and *press on.*

One thing means we need to be single-minded and focused on what we're trying to accomplish. There is a time for multitasking, but multitasking is definitely a distraction from one primary goal.

Forgetting indicates putting something out of our minds. We need to clear our minds of less important things so we can be free to do what is most important.

Reaching forward involves stretching or extending ourselves. At times I feel as if I'm trying to do something that's out of reach or out of my comfort zone, but the more I stretch toward the goal, the closer I come to achieving it.

Press on means to go forward with effort and commitment. Worthwhile changes aren't simply going to happen. They must be pursued with determination, perseverance, and intentionality.

Remember that self-discipline, which is also known as self-control, is one of God's promises in the fruit of the Spirit (Galatians 5:22-23). Self-control comes as a result of God's Spirit living within us. That sure is a good reminder that He will help us through the power of His Spirit within us.

"Now glory be to God, who by his mighty power at work within us is able to do far more than we would ever dare to ask or even dream of" (Ephesians 3:20, TLB).

God doesn't see us with our self-imposed limitations. He sees us with the potential and ability to change and grow in every area of our lives. He gives us the confidence to achieve and accomplish, to do and to be, and to move forward with life.

God is not a life coach; He is a life changer.

Now you know the first step for making any kind of change in life takes self-discipline. I like the way Jim Rohn says it: "Discipline is the bridge between goals and accomplishment."[2]

I have often admired a friend's self-discipline and perseverance. After moving to Phoenix while in her forties, she went back to school for her college degree. I encourage you to think and reflect on any area of your life that you feel might need discipline so you can accomplish something either personal or spiritual. This may be just the right time to turn over that new leaf.

For God has not given us a spirit of timidity, but of power
and love and discipline.
2 TIMOTHY 1:7

Be a Trailblazer

Let's start to blaze a trail with some goal setting. It'll be a lot easier
knowing we are doing it together.

A goal should be:

- specific
- measurable
- achievable
- valuable
- rewarded

These are some markers along the trail to help us as we pursue our
goals. Ready, set, go!

Marker 1. Write it down! About 80 percent of all goals are accomplished if they are written down. Otherwise, you don't have a goal—
you only have a wish. When you see a goal written down, it becomes
a reality. (Specific: I'm going to write down exactly how much weight
I want to lose by a specific date.)

Marker 2. Have a plan! Without a specific plan, you'll find it difficult to reach your goal. (Measurable: I will walk three times a week [or
do some form of exercise], be more conscious of ingredients on food
labels, and watch my fat intake.)

Marker 3. Take it one day at a time! Trying to achieve everything
at once can be overwhelming and defeating. (Achievable: I'll focus on
what I've accomplished each day instead of how difficult it might be
overall.)

Marker 4. Don't give up! It will be worth it in the long run. Keep
your ultimate goal in mind. (Valuable: Even if I mess up one day, I'll
get back on track the next day.)

Marker 5. Be good to yourself! When you reach your goal, you deserve a reward. (When I lose five pounds, I'll celebrate!)

Think back to a year ago. What changes do you see in yourself? How has God used those changes in and through your life? Now think about moving forward. What self-discipline will it take to reach your goal?

Henry David Thoreau said, "Go ahead and build your castles in the air. That's where they belong. Now put some foundations under them."[3]

Goals of the Heart

After a move, you can make changes not only in your personal life but in your spiritual life as well. Some of the most significant goals I've made are spiritual ones. They are the goals from my heart. A spiritual goal brings glory to God, bears fruit of the Holy Spirit, and is built on hope, not hopelessness. Of course our ultimate goal should be oneness with God, to be the best we can be for Him, to learn more of Him, and to walk daily with Him.

When we relocated to Phoenix, I wanted to read and study the Bible all the more. I had come to a different place and stage in my life, and I found that certain verses, no matter how many times I had read them in the past, had new meaning after we moved. I wanted to find a Bible study where I could grow by digging into God's Word and building community with other women. I wanted to cultivate a more faithful prayer time.

Take a good look at *your* heart. Are there any changes that need to take place? Why don't you take a minute and think of three spiritual goals and three personal goals you would like to achieve.

Think not just about what you will do; think about who you will become in the process.

The Heart of the Matter

Let's go a little deeper into the heart of the matter. In Joseph Allison's book *Setting Goals That Count*, he talks about how God influences your goal setting and plan making through your internal guidance system, which the Bible refers to as the heart.[4] God guides you through your heart.

The Bible reveals that your internal guidance system has two inter-related functions. The heart function refers to setting goals and forming character. The mind function deals with making daily plans to reach your goals. See the difference between a person's heart and mind in this verse: "I will put My laws into their minds, and I will write them on their hearts. And I will be their God, and they shall be My people" (Hebrews 8:10).

Notice that it says God will *put* (suggesting temporary keeping) His laws into their minds, and *write* (suggesting permanent keeping) them on their hearts. We often say that we've changed our minds, but seldom do we say we've changed our hearts. A person's heart directs his or her mind. Jesus taught that the heart guides our entire lives (see Matthew 12:34; Mark 7:21-23; Luke 6:43-45). It's the switchboard for our thoughts, feelings, and actions. If we allow God to change our hearts, we change our entire lives. God can transform our lives by giving us new hearts for Him, as well as a new purpose that is achievable with new goals.

A Changed Heart

From the moment Laurie walked into our Moving On After Moving In study, skepticism was written all over her face. She couldn't quite figure out whether or not we were for real. Laurie had never experienced unconditional love, and she didn't exactly know how to accept it. She had heard of Jesus Christ but didn't know Him personally. She asked me to come over to her house weekly, "just to answer some questions," she said. She talked; I listened. I talked; she listened. We read Scripture. We prayed. But I could tell that her heart just wasn't ready. She couldn't accept how simple and uncomplicated the love of Christ actually is.

She quit coming to class, but we kept calling her. She always had an excuse for not coming. Finally she said there was no point in our meeting anymore, so we stopped. Occasionally I saw her in the grocery store, but that was all the contact we had.

One morning two years later, the phone rang, and it was Laurie. "Can I come over?" she said. "I have something to tell you."

When Laurie walked in the front door, I could see it all over her face. She was a different person. She smiled and embraced me. "I just had to see you," she said. "You see, I started going to this small church nearby, and then I got involved in a Bible study, and now I know Christ!" By this time my eyes were brimming with tears. "The reason I had to see you was to ask for your forgiveness."

"My forgiveness?"

"Yes," she said. "All of you were so loving and kind to me in our study, and my heart was so hardened. And then you wouldn't give up on me, and you put up with all my rebellion against God. I know God has forgiven me, and I want you to forgive me too."

"Oh, Laurie," I said, and we both started to cry. "Yes, of course I'll forgive you."

The change was so obvious; it showed in her eyes, her smile, and her voice. I was touched by her desire to seek my forgiveness.

She left that day and I haven't seen her since. But I was once again reminded of God's powerful, life-changing love and how, in some small way, He allowed me to be a part of Laurie's journey to find Him.

Heart to Heart

"I think I can, I think I can," said the Little Engine That Could. Before you start huffing and puffing to make changes, to become more self-disciplined, or to set new goals, let me share some thoughts to keep you on track.

You are starting over with an empty calendar. You aren't over-committed, and you don't have a hectic schedule—yet. Choose carefully how you fill your calendar. Now is the time to take a good look at what you put back into your life. It's a good time to make different choices than you have in the past. Perhaps you need to check your priorities and make sure they are in the right order. You can choose to unclutter and uncomplicate your life. Perhaps you were too busy before you moved. What a great time to evaluate what's most important to you.

When I feel myself getting off track with my life, I know I need to "come back to center." My "center" is God. When everything pivots around Him, I'm on track. When I try to fit Him around everything else, my life is out of balance. Oswald Chambers said, "Always keep your life measured by the standards of Jesus."[5]

Doing more doesn't always make you a more productive person; it can make you a more exhausted person! Ask yourself if what you are doing is right for you, your marriage, and your family.

Being busy isn't necessarily being better. Maybe you just need to step back and take a deep breath before you plunge into life again. It's good for your soul to stop and smell the flowers, to watch a sunset.

Be who you are and strive to be the best you.

Don't waste a single move—grow, learn, and change.

Understand that you don't have to have it all together. Just try to remember where you put what you've got. (My spices aren't organized alphabetically, and not all my pictures are in photo albums.)

Unpack Your Survival Box

Some practical tips to help your life run smoothly and to be more organized:

- Establish a family message center. Use it for shopping lists, phone messages, calendars, reminders.
- Use plastic ice-cube trays to store earrings in your jewelry drawer.
- Attach jewelry pins to an old T-shirt and keep it on a hanger. Hang necklaces on wooden pegs.
- Put cardboard between sets of placemats so you can remove one set without disturbing the others.
- Hang tablecloths on oversize sturdy, padded hangers.
- Store napkin rings by sets in ziplock bags.
- Store socks, belts, gloves, scarves, stockings, and underwear in pocketed shoe bags.
- Invest in an assortment of hooks, dividers, clear boxes, and other containers that make it easy to keep things separate and quick to find.

- Using colorful file folders, create a file for everything you're interested in and involved in—from A to Z. My files start with antiques and end with weddings.
- Use the space under a skirted table to store things. I put small things under there that have to be temporarily relocated to make room for Christmas decorations.
- Add an extra shelf in any unused space at the top of the closet.
- Add another garment pole in your closet above the existing one for hanging shorter items like blouses or skirts.
- One of the best ways to declutter is the three-box or three-bag method. Designate your items as (1) give away, (2) put away, and (3) throw away. The challenge is to do what each one says!
- Hang a shoe organizer in the garage. My daughter keeps all her kids' sports shoes and flip-flops in designated pockets for easy access on the way to a game or outdoors.

Every Sunday night I take stock of what I have to do that week: check my calendar, make a to-do list in my phone, and make note of e-mails I need to answer, calls I have to make, or appointments and meetings that are on my schedule. That way I have a jump start on my week and feel organized.

Are you moving in the right direction? You'll know in the next chapter.

CHAPTER 17

A MOVE IN THE RIGHT DIRECTION

I find the great thing in this world is not so much where we stand, as in what direction we are moving.

OLIVER WENDELL HOLMES

WHEN I WAS A YOUNG GIRL, Mama and I went on a trip to South Carolina. We stopped at a little country gas station in the middle of nowhere. An old gentleman was sitting in a chair in front of the station. Mama rolled down the window and said, "Excuse me, sir. Could you tell me how much farther it is?"

He scratched his head as he replied, "Well, ma'am, it all depends on where you're comin' from and where you're goin' to." She realized how funny her question was and we all laughed together. Mama then gave him the missing information, and he told her how far we had to go.

His words often come back to my mind. I ask myself every now and then, *Where am I comin' from and where am I goin' to?* This keeps me focused on making sure I'm moving in the right direction. Since our journey together will be coming to an end soon, let me ask you, "Do you know where you're goin' to, and are you movin' in the right direction?"

Oswald Chambers puts it all in perspective. "It is of no use to pray for the old days; stand square where you are and make the present better than any past has been. Base all on your relationship to God and go forward, and presently you will find that what is emerging is infinitely better than the past ever was."[1]

Write that down and put it on your refrigerator! One of my prayers for you is that your move is, or will be, "infinitely better than the past ever was."

Following Our Leader

Who we are and the decisions we make are affected by where we come from and the life we've led. But one thing is sure: you're moving in the right direction if you're following the Leader, Jesus Christ. To know Him is to love Him, and to follow Him is life changing.

As Christians, we are to "follow God's example in everything [we] do" (Ephesians 5:1, TLB). Our Leader, Jesus, beckons us to follow Him. Jesus said, "Come, follow Me" (Matthew 19:21). The more you read, study, observe, and understand the life of Christ—and then imitate Him—the more He will flow from you. *In all you do and say, "live out Jesus" in your life.*

By following Jesus and living a Christ-centered life, your focus will shift from your world to the world of others. By refocusing, you are taking another step in the process of moving forward—another step in the right direction.

Martha! Get Out of That Kitchen!

I can't tell you how many times I've heard over the years, "Susan, get out of that kitchen and come here! You've got to hear (or see) this!" Whether it's the kitchen, backyard, or garage, we've all been absorbed somewhere else when something good was going on.

I can certainly relate to the story of sisters Mary and Martha, as told in Luke 10:38-42. Here's how it all played out:

Martha had invited Jesus to dinner at the home she shared with

Mary, her younger sister, and their brother, Lazarus. I'm sure their home was swept, dusted, cleaned, and tidy. Martha wanted everything just right for Jesus. She might have had candles lit and fresh flowers on the table. (Oh, how many times I've spent the whole day getting my house ready for friends coming for dinner!)

Martha seemed to be preoccupied and worried about every detail. She wanted to please Jesus, to serve Him, and, of course, to do the right thing for Him. In the back of her mind, she was probably thinking about how important it was to be the perfect hostess. She was far too caught up in the details of *doing* and lost sight of the importance of just *being* with Jesus. She was missing out on the gift of His presence.

While Martha was busy in the kitchen with preparations, Mary was in the other room listening to Jesus. How could her sister be sitting in there, relaxing and just listening, when there was so much to do? I can imagine that Martha angrily marched out of the kitchen, ready to let everyone know she was knocking herself out doing everything, while they were all enjoying themselves.

Well, you can imagine what happened next as the stress and pressure of preparation came to a head. Martha was ticked off and chose to vent to Jesus! She said, "Doesn't it seem unfair to you that my sister just sits here while I do all the work? Tell her to come and help me" (Luke 10:40, TLB).

He didn't rebuke Martha. Instead Jesus replied calmly, "Martha, dear friend, you are so upset over all these details! There is really only one thing worth being concerned about. Mary has discovered it—and I won't take it away from her" (Luke 10:41-42, TLB). The one thing that Mary had discovered was that spending time *with* Jesus was far more important than the busyness of doing things *for* Jesus.

Notice that Jesus didn't get upset with Martha for what she was doing. There was no doubt that she had a servant's heart. She just needed an attitude and a priority adjustment. (Oh yes, Lord—so many times I do too!) Whereas Martha was task-oriented, Mary was

Master-oriented. Martha was interested in what she needed to get done; Mary was interested in who she was becoming.

In *Between Walden and the Whirlwind*, Jean Fleming says, "The Christian life should have a rhythm of doing and resting, speaking and listening, giving and receiving." She goes on to say, "Not only must God minister through us, He must minister to us."[2]

Give some serious thought about the rhythm of your life and who you are becoming as you start over in a different and new place. Keep in mind the Martha and Mary story.

Martha's Hands and Mary's Heart

As you begin to settle in, move forward, and build community connections, you will become more involved in the lives of others. Remember the importance of balancing the work of Martha's hands as she served, with the gift of Mary's heart as she sat and listened. A balance of both allows God to minister *through* you and *to* you.

These are some of the ways you can reach out, get involved, and build relationships as you put into practice Martha's hands with Mary's heart:

Put the welcome mat out. "Be hospitable to one another" (1 Peter 4:9). Genuine hospitality involves opening your heart and your home, selflessly sharing yourself and what you have. Hospitality begins in conversation, in encounter, in eye contact, in attentive listening. It's about people, not preparation.

Hospitality is:

- Reaching out
- Inviting in
- Gathering together
- A place for laughter and tears
- A place of acceptance and warmth
- A place to share, to be listened to, and to be heard
- Saying, "You are welcome here." "My house may not be in order, but come anyway." "What I have is yours."

No matter the occasion—gathering friends together for coffee, conversation, or a meal; offering your home overnight; hosting a Bible study; or inviting kids over after school—put that welcome mat outside your front door (you do have one, don't you?), and open your arms wide as you convey the love of Christ to others.

Consider this: If a new family has moved to your neighborhood, invite them over for a casual cookout, along with other neighbors to meet and greet.

Come alongside someone. "If one falls, the other pulls him up" (Ecclesiastes 4:10, TLB).

Look around you. What can you do to come alongside someone who needs a helping hand in your new community or church? Do you see a need? Then fill it! The smallest gesture can be huge to someone in need. Someone could be right under your nose—on the same street or in the same apartment or condo complex—someone who needs to know she is not alone. When a person or a situation tugs at your heart, act on it.

A newcomer in our Moving On study had recently moved here when she heard that a single woman, who didn't know anyone, needed a ride to chemotherapy each week. She came alongside her, took her to all the chemo treatments, and stayed with her during the infusions. Be an extension of Christ's love to someone in need.

Consider this: Offer to take a couple of meals to a new mom just home from the hospital, or make a grocery run for her.

It takes a little encouragement. "Encourage one another and build up one another" (1 Thessalonians 5:11).

Encouragement is the act of inspiring others with renewed courage, a renewed spirit, and a renewed hope. It can be as simple as an act of kindness, a note of reassurance, a word of cheer, or a gesture of support. It's intentionally doing or saying something to build someone up. Some things I love to say to encourage others include: "I believe in you," "You can do it," and "I'm your biggest fan."

One of the things you might not know about me is that pom-poms are one way I like to encourage people. I love to shake them as I cheer on my family and friends—even strangers—to victory in what they want to do or be. I even keep them in my car. You never know when someone in the course of my day might need some encouragement. I know it sounds a little crazy, but I'm just that kind of girl!

Reflect the encouragement of Christ, just as He encourages you.

Consider this: Send a card or a note encouraging your pastor, a teacher, or anyone who has made a difference in your life.

How can I serve you? "But the greatest among you shall be your servant" (Matthew 23:11).

It's pretty amazing that Jesus—*Jesus!*—actually knelt down with a basin and a towel to wash the disciples' stinky, dusty, dirty feet.

We did that in a small group once during a study about being a servant. It was a humbling and uncomfortable experience. But sometimes that's what serving is all about: humbling yourself to do something that's out of your comfort zone or that makes you sweat a little.

It's not always glamorous.

It's not always center stage.

Sometimes it's in the kitchen cooking a meal, or staying behind to clean up after everyone's left, or changing a poopy diaper in the church nursery. Sometimes it's a thankless job that's hard work and a sacrifice of your time and energy. But go ahead and do it anyway; give yourself as a gift to others. If Jesus can do it, so can you.

Consider this: Offer to help unpack boxes when someone new has moved in with small children, or better yet, offer to babysit.

Be with me. "You will give me back my life and give me wonderful joy in your presence" (Acts 2:28, TLB).

Jesus' example is one of sharing life with His disciples. He wanted them to be with Him. They spent three years doing life together.

Today, though we live in a world of people longing to connect, we are alienated from each other. In crowds of people, we are lonely. We go to church but are uninvolved. We wave to our neighbors but don't take the time to get to know them. Our emptiness is filled with busyness instead of relationships.

We have a "being with" crisis in our communities, in our neighborhoods, and even in our families.

But you can choose to stop that pattern. When you make new friends, take time to get to know them well. Get together one-on-one and ask your new friend to tell you her story. Everyone has a story.

Simply be with your friend, your husband, and your children. Sometimes that's all it takes to close the gap of loneliness, the space of emptiness, and the longing to be connected.

Consider this: Visit someone who has been uprooted and moved to an assisted-living facility.

Just show up! "Go and get him and comfort him" (Genesis 21:18, TLB).

We hadn't been in Phoenix long when Mama called to tell me Daddy was in the hospital having tests for chest pain. She said not to come—the results weren't back, and we didn't know whether it was serious or not. My daddy had never been seriously ill and had never been in the hospital. I thought about it all day, talked it over with Bill that evening, and made a decision: I would hop on a plane to Florida the next day to be with them during long days of testing.

I wanted to surprise Daddy with my visit, so I didn't tell them I was coming. I caught a cab to the hospital, walked down the long corridor to his room, and peeked around the door. He was sitting up on a steel gurney, with wires attached all over his chest, gazing up at the ceiling. "Surprise!" I said as I practically jumped into the room.

He looked at me, wide-eyed, with a smile covering his whole face, and said, "I'm so glad you came!"

I'll never forget that moment and never regret my decision to "just show up."

No gifts, no balloons, no pom-poms, no flowers—just me, just my presence.

Just showing up in someone's life can make the difference between hope and despair, laughter and tears, calm and anxiety, happiness and sadness. All it takes is *you.*

Consider this: Show up by celebrating the birthday of a newcomer who may not know anyone nearby. (It could be someone from work, church, or your neighborhood.)

Listen to my heart speak. "A wise man listens to others" (Proverbs 12:15, TLB).

You recognize the telltale signs: sadness in her eyes, shoulders drooping from the weight of the world, tears close to the surface. Her world has turned upside down. She's been uprooted by a major life change and has lost her sense of self and purpose. You know the feeling—you've been there, or maybe you still are.

She has an insatiable need for someone to listen as her pain pours out in words that may ramble. She needs someone who will not just listen without judgment but with a compassionate, sensitive heart. Someone who will show love and care by listening to the cry of her heart.

Jesus loved enough and cared enough to listen to the brokenhearted and the lonely. Just as He bent His knee to serve the disciples, He bends His ear to listen to us. "I love the Lord because he hears my prayers. . . . he bends down and listens" (Psalm 116:1-2, TLB).

Will you be that "someone" now?

Consider this: When a new friend is going through a tough transition after moving, listen to her story with an understanding heart. You might be a step further down the road of adjustment than she is.

Give to my need. "It is more blessed to give than to receive" (Acts 20:35).

Once upon a time, a friend showed up at my door with two bags full of frozen food from her freezer. Bill had been in a car accident and had been out of work for a long time. Our kitchen pantry and refrigerator were rather bare. As we would say, "It was slim pickin's at our house." I was quite taken by what she said as she handed me the bags. It went something like this: "Will you do me a favor and take this frozen food? I have just cleaned out my freezer and it would really help me if you could use it." I was floored. She had seen our need and gave to us out of her abundance—without embarrassing or humiliating me. The manner and words she chose were kind, sensitive, and gracious. She truly made me feel like I was helping *her*.

There are different ways to meet a person's needs. It might be food on the table, clothes for the closet, needed home repairs, yard maintenance, babysitting—you name it. It could be financial support for a church, a ministry, a missionary, or another worthy cause. Or an anonymous gift to help out a family or a friend. When you see a need, do whatever you can—just do something, in the name of Jesus.

Consider this: There is someone who needs to be included in your Bible study or other activity. She might need a ride to get there too.

If you look back over each idea for reaching out, you'll see they all reflect how Jesus did it. He didn't just *tell* us what to do; He *demonstrated* it. He *lived it out*. We've talked about this before. You know I'm big on living out Scripture and biblical principles. Otherwise, how would anyone know who we are—and *whose* we are?

You see, it's not about bringing attention to ourselves; it's about the overflow of His presence in our lives. It's saying, "I am a follower of Christ and I belong to Him."

How do you begin?

- Be available. Let people know you have the time and desire to help out. They won't know if you don't tell them.

- Be aware. Put up your antennae. Observe and listen to people and situations around you. Be sensitive to what is going on in people's lives.

- Ask, don't assume. Assumptions aren't always correct. Ask *what* the specific need is, ask *how* you might best help, ask *when* the best time would be to get together. (If you are simply going to "show up," make sure the timing is right.)

- Be accepting. Don't judge a person from the outside until you know her on the inside. There's always more to someone than meets the eye. She might look like she has it all together, but not many of us do.

- Take action. If God nudges you to do something, do it. Consider it a prompting from the Holy Spirit. Don't put it off and end up regretting that you did nothing or find that it's too late to do anything.

God will do incredible things in you and through you as you begin to move forward. Just watch and see.

Heart to Heart

You've come so far! I want to celebrate you—the person you are and the person you are becoming. Allow me to tell you how glad I am that you read this book. We've become good friends through these chapters. You probably didn't realize we had so much in common, did you?

You'll make it through this time of transition because you have so much going for you. You've got me in your corner, and I'll be praying for you. You have an amazing God who loves you unconditionally and will never leave you. You've got a fresh start with each new day. You're beginning to bloom!

I pray that you sense God's peace and hope for tomorrow. You can now look ahead and move forward.

As you move forward, the next three chapters will give you insight into the world of millennial movers (you may be one!), military movers, and the impact of being uprooted by other major life changes. You'll also find suggestions for encouraging and reaching out to people in these circumstances.

In addition, as a result of meeting thousands of uprooted women through my speaking and teaching opportunities, I'm able to give you a glimpse of the changes in the last twenty years that have affected movers today, as well as a window into who your new neighbors might be. Good things for you to know!

CHAPTER 18

THE NEW REALITY

*Do not waste time bothering whether you "love" your
neighbor; act as if you did. . . . When you are behaving as if
you loved someone, you will presently come to love him.*
C. S. LEWIS

I THINK IT WOULD BE safe to say that, in the past twenty years, the
mover's options have changed and expanded tremendously.

Changes in the economy, in technology, and in popular lifestyles
have had a big impact on individuals and families as they move. Some
changes are for the better, while some have made relocating more
difficult.

The cost of living has increased. This has a direct influence on the
freedom to improve one's lifestyle by making a move and the ability to
buy a newer or larger home.

Interest rates are lower. This is a good thing for home buyers now,
but as you know, nothing remains the same!

*Communication has expanded our sources of information and
knowledge about the "who, what, and where" of relocating.* We now
have instant and easy access to anything, anywhere, anytime. This can
be a two-edged sword. Easy access to information about a city, country,

climate, churches, business opportunities, or schools can help make relocation decisions easier, but information overload can also make them more difficult.

Social networking bridges the miles but can disconnect us from personal contact. With social media, texting, and e-mailing at our fingertips, we are prone to disregard the need for building community and investing in personal, face-to-face relationships.

Technology allows people to work anywhere in the world from home. With a cell phone, computer, or tablet, you can live practically anywhere and conduct business from your home office, kitchen, or patio. A "movable home business" is a growing trend. It's not uncommon for families to move often since their jobs can be taken with them. As adventurous as this is, it's often hard for the family to put down roots and make lasting friendships.

Sacrificing one career to follow the career of another is not uncommon today. In a two-income family, one spouse must often give up a secure career to follow his or her spouse for the new job. This scenario may qualify a positive move, but it can have a negative effect on the marriage relationship.

Your New Neighbors

Today's global mobility and connectivity make it more likely that the ethnicity and background of your neighbors will be more diverse than ever before. Here's a little insight into some of your new neighbors and ways that you and I can reach out to them. You might even recognize yourself in these faces, and I might be knocking on your door!

Your new neighbors could be from another country and speak a different language. Their religion, food, social behavior, clothing, and music could be different from yours. I encourage you to see this as an opportunity to broaden your appreciation for other cultures! Be open to learning about other customs, countries, and traditions from your neighbors. It's easy to research online an appropriate small gift, food, or greeting for a family who moves into your community from another country or culture.

A young woman who moved here from another country and culture recently came into my life. I found out what kind of tea was popular in her country and gave her some as a welcome gift. After our relationship began to grow, I gave her a Bible. A cup of tea opened the door to our friendship and introduced her to our community and to Jesus.

The family next door might not be "traditional." Twenty years ago, a family consisting of two biological parents with two children would likely have been your neighbors. Today, the new family moving in might have one parent, stepparents, stepchildren, two mamas, two daddies, foster parents, or unmarried parents. Their lifestyle and value system may be entirely different from yours, but that shouldn't stop you from reaching out to them.

Invite a new family to neighborhood block parties or to community picnic potlucks. Include them in some of your family activities or social events. Have a neighborhood drop-in to meet and greet. It can be as casual as setting up a table and chairs outside in the garage or driveway on a Saturday morning and inviting the neighbors to stop by for coffee and donuts. Be inclusive, following the example of Jesus.

Retiring baby boomers are on the move. Many retirees want to be near family or live in a warm climate or a retirement community. They may be downsizing their homes and possessions and leaving behind friends, community involvement, and independence. The adjustment can often be much harder than they anticipated.

A former CFO of a global Fortune 500 company told me that he used to make decisions about allocating millions of dollars for his company. He went on to confess that, since his retirement, his biggest decision was choosing what kind of cereal he would eat each morning. It was obvious that he struggled with a loss of identity and significance in his life.

Retirees often have time and resources to volunteer in the church or community or to serve as consultants in their areas of expertise. Don't assume that every retiree wants to spend his or her days on the golf course. You may be able to connect her to a volunteer opportunity that leads to a fulfilling new stage in life.

Idealistic millennials (born between 1981 and 1995) are more likely to be renting in an urban area. You'll find them enthusiastically building community and relationships in their corner of the city—for now. They aren't likely to stay put long. Millennials want to be free and unencumbered to travel and relocate when the opportunity arises.

I have many younger friends who come and go in my life with their wanderlust lifestyles. I have found that meeting them on their own turf—a local bistro or coffee shop—is a great way to get acquainted. Especially when I pick up the tab!

The short-term mover has followed the temporary job. Short-term contracts and temporary consulting work are on the rise. Like the millennials, short-term movers will probably be your leasing neighbors.

A lifestyle of contract or consulting work can create a sense of detachment, of not belonging anywhere. It's important to invest in these short-term neighbors. Your friendliness may become a turning point in their lives.

When my condo-living friends meet new, short-term neighbors, they give them a list of local services, favorite restaurants, and things to do in the area. "It really helps them get on the fast track with learning the area," they say.

The number of single movers is increasing. The single professional, single parent, and divorced or widowed woman is often on her own as she faces the daunting task of relocation. The stress of decision making, finding a place to live, and moving her belongings can be overwhelming and are only a few of the difficult tasks she must face by herself.

A retired couple made it their mission to come alongside new single movers in their church. They gave their phone number to a widow who had moved to their community so she would have someone to call in case of an emergency. The husband offered to cut her grass, and his wife planted some flowers in the woman's yard. When they met a young single mom with two children, they offered to give her a ride to church. They demonstrate the love of Jesus to these and other singles.

The multigenerational household is making a comeback. More families are moving to accommodate aging parents, grandparents, or grandchildren. They come together to take care of their family, to reduce the cost of living, and to face life together.

A friend reached out to a new multigenerational family on her street by taking the elderly and ill grandparents to doctor appointments. She prayed for them in the car before each appointment and continued to pray for them as she became aware of their other needs. A bond of friendship evolved and eventually she began to offer encouraging Scripture passages during difficult times. Prayer and Scripture—a pretty good combination, don't you think?

Since you probably still think of yourself as a newcomer too, you know what it feels like to be the new person on the block. You know from your experience what you wish someone would say or do for you. Think about that when you meet one of the new faces in your community.

Won't you be my neighbor?
Won't you please, won't you please,
Please won't you be my neighbor?
THEME SONG FROM *MISTER ROGERS' NEIGHBORHOOD*

One day I noticed the For Sale sign was gone from the yard of the house down the street. A few weeks later I saw the moving van arrive with all the furniture and brown boxes. A car pulled up in the driveway and three children ran with excitement into the house that would soon become their home. Someone who appeared to be the grandmother stayed in the car. A woman got out of the driver's seat and slowly made her way up the sidewalk to the front door. She turned to look up and down the street and to make a quick assessment of her new yard. It was obvious she was surveying the neighborhood as well as the yard work that needed to be done.

I imagined her story: a single working mom, three children, and a grandmother who will live with them to help care for the children.

As I watched from the window, I looked at her with eyes of understanding and with memories all too familiar. Once you've gone through a move, you don't forget the feelings that come with being the new family in the neighborhood. It seemed as if I could read her thoughts at that moment: *Who are my neighbors? Will we have anything in common? Will they like us? Will anyone come over to meet us?* I knew immediately what I was going to do.

First, this was an opportunity to reach out to a woman who was new to our neighborhood at a vulnerable time in her life. Second, I had been there many times as a mover and understood what she was going through. I knew what she needed.

Been There, Felt That

You, my friends, know what my new neighbor was probably thinking and feeling, and what she would eventually have to deal with:

> Facing the unknown
> Coping with the unfamiliar
> Starting all over again
> Leaving behind family and friends
> Making new friends
> Dealing with loneliness

These are the timeless issues and challenges that come with being uprooted. We have talked about each one in this book. You know about them all too well. The old saying "Some things never change" still holds true.

A Bridge of Connection

It should be no surprise that the face of our culture and lifestyle in America is changing and will continue to change as we "move" into the future. Yet even though we live in a changing world, we know our God is unchanging. "Jesus Christ is the same yesterday, today, and forever" (Hebrews 13:8, TLB). I never get tired of reading that verse. It brings strength and stability to my world.

We need to be His hands to serve, His feet to walk in love, His voice of truth, and His listening ear. We need to get on with the business of being neighbors who exemplify the love of Jesus.

As followers of Christ, we are compelled to love our neighbors and live in community with them. We are to demonstrate the love of Christ in ways our neighbors can see through our actions, feel through our behavior, and hear through our words. Throughout the New Testament, Jesus demonstrates this over and over again through His actions and words. Our role is simply to bear witness to God's truth in word and deed. Only God's Spirit, however, can compel someone to receive the message of Christ.

Don't Judge a Book by Its Cover

When I read Cyndi's story below, I was reminded of how often I have prejudged and stereotyped people based on their outer appearances rather than their hearts. Oh, Lord, forgive me. May I always build a bridge of connection with love and acceptance rather than a wall of judgment.

> The neighborhood we moved into was wonderful. All of our
> neighbors greeted us with kindness and welcoming arms.
> We spent many hours at the playground together with our
> children. I was convinced that at least a few of them had to
> be Christians, but after being more exposed to their lifestyles,
> I discovered that none of them was Christian.
>
> If I had met my neighbors and had noticed their
> concealed tattoos and body piercings, or heard some of their
> vulgar language and music, or realized that we were the
> only ones who didn't drink alcohol, I think I would have
> locked myself and my young, impressionable children in
> our apartment, never to see sunlight again.
>
> However, God covered my eyes and did not allow me
> to see this right away. He allowed me to see friendly, caring

people who loved their children and wanted what was best for them.

A few women persuaded me to go to the gym with them, and I began to love and care for them—and enjoy their company. They soon learned about my walk with Christ, and though they might not have agreed, they respected my faith and did not ban me from the group. This was good because I wanted to share Christ with all of them and sow a seed in each of their lives.

God began to open my eyes to my own prejudice and stereotyping. If God had not covered my eyes, I would have prejudged these women who, without prompting, had ministered to me, a newcomer.

I hope that despite all the stereotypes, taboos, and prejudices in our society, I will always remember to look at people as God's creations and souls He wants to claim.

May you and I strive to look at our neighbors through the eyes of Jesus.

Be wise in the way you live around those who are not Christians. Make good use of your time. Speak with them in such a way they will want to listen to you. . . . Know how to give the right answer to anyone.
COLOSSIANS 4:5-6, NLV

Remember Jesus' command to "love your neighbor as yourself" (Luke 10:27, NLT).

Here are a few golden rules for welcoming a new neighbor:

- Just show up!
- Treat others the same way you want them to treat you (see Luke 6:31).
- Be inclusive, not exclusive.

- Listen to their stories.
- Be warm and friendly—smile and wave when you see them.
- Be kind, thoughtful, and considerate—it's contagious.
- Remember their names and the names of their children. Write them down if you need to.
- Don't overstay on the first visit.
- Once is not enough—connect again.
- Don't forget—invite them to your church!

Don't let being a newcomer keep you from doing and saying the things that will impact another life for Christ. You may be the very person God will use to "move" that new neighbor closer to Jesus. Remember these beautiful words, widely attributed to Teresa of Avila:

Christ has no body now on earth but yours.
No hands, no feet on earth but yours.
Yours are the eyes through which he looks compassion on this world.
Yours are the feet with which he walks to do good.
Yours are the hands through which he blesses all the world.
Yours are the hands, yours are the feet,
Yours are the eyes, you are his body.
Christ has no body now on earth but yours.

CHAPTER 19

A MILITARY PCS MEANS MOVE

See, I am sending an Angel before you to lead you safely to
the land I have prepared for you.

EXODUS 23:20, TLB

IN THE FIRST FEW MINUTES, I fell in love with the uniform, but the man who was wearing it stole my heart for a lifetime.

Not only did I marry a military man; my daddy was active-duty military and wore a uniform for twenty-five years before he retired. Daddy served during World War II and the Korean War. Bill and my brother served during the Vietnam War. My brother looked pretty good in his uniform too, even if he was my brother.

No wonder I love the military so much.

The military was, and always will be, a part of who I am. I am still overcome with pride and patriotism when I see Air Force, Army, Marine, or Navy service members. I love what they represent and still love their uniforms.

When Daddy was stationed halfway around the world, I remember Mama being anxious and worried when she didn't hear from him for weeks or months at a time. I remember her playing their favorite love

213

songs on the record player and sobbing in fear that he might not return home from war.

I remember Bill's dedication as a medic when he worked passionately to help heal the bodies and minds of those who were wounded and broken in Vietnam. It was a world of pain and suffering that a young recruit right out of high school never imagined he would see.

I know God wastes nothing. If you know Him and desire to please Him, He will bring your life full circle for His glory. He will use what you've experienced, what you've learned, and what you know to reach out to others, encourage them, and pass on His hope.

He did that with my daddy, a man who served others with a quiet and gentle spirit until he died. He did that with my brother, who always offers his time and a helping hand to others. And He did that with my Bill. From his background, Bill gained enormous insight, wisdom, and discernment into emotional pain and brokenness. God blessed him with the gift to counsel, teach, and bring hope to countless hurting people throughout his life.

Through Just Moved Ministry, God has given me the privilege to do just that in the lives of military spouses all over the world. I am in my sweet spot of ministry when I can teach, encourage, listen to, pray for, and be with these women.

From year to year, I see many of them again in different parts of the world and at different military installations. I have great compassion and sensitivity for military spouses and women on active duty. They have become my friends and I have become their cheerleader.

You can do the same thing. When you meet a military spouse or active duty member, be her cheerleader, love her, pray for her, and encourage her.

My Heroes

Let me introduce you to the life of the military spouse and her family as I know them in today's military world.

These wives and moms juggle the endless home responsibilities while their men are deployed, just returning from deployment, or getting ready to go again. Many men are gone for months on TDY (temporary duty) or training missions.

Their wives live between welcoming them home and telling them good-bye. They live with the reality that some of their men will come home with post-traumatic stress disorder (PTSD) or the loss of a limb. Others won't come home at all.

They live each day with fear of the unknown, loneliness from long separations, emotional highs and lows, and the stress of managing homes, finances, and children on their own. The pressure and stress wears heavily on them and, over time, has a ripple effect on their marriages and parenting.

Military spouses all over the world tell me it's not uncommon for them to PCS (permanent change of station) on an average of once every three years.

Imagine moving every three years. Imagine that your spouse is deployed or on assignment. Alone, you must pack the boxes, oversee the movers, sell the house, handle endless details, comfort and parent the children, tell a community of military friends good-bye, and settle into yet another new military installation or community. Imagine knowing no one. All those outside of the military have no clue what you're going through. You're weary from worry, worn-out from trying to hold yourself and everything else together, and overwhelmed when the car and the washing machine break down at the same time. Now imagine carrying these burdens after a move overseas when you don't speak the language and housing at your duty station is not available.

All of this is just the tip of the iceberg for the stress-filled life of the military spouse.

Never forget that many wives and moms are active-duty military themselves, and they face the emotions and separation of leaving their families behind when they deploy. Spouses or family members have to step up and take on full-time care for their children. Can you imagine the emotions of a mom leaving her children behind? Imagine wondering if the everyday details of her family members' lives will be taken care of while she takes care of the big details of serving her country.

A Fighting Spirit

Yet, in spite of all these things, *many military spouses live with a resilient spirit of hope, perseverance, and optimism that defines the life that comes with being a military wife and mom.*

This is what I've observed:

- Military spouses have a determination to rise above their circumstances.
- They cling to their faith and trust in God instead of giving up or losing hope.
- They rely on God's Word to keep their world from crumbling in times of despair.
- They put their own needs last and the needs of another military sister in distress first.
- They are physically exhausted from another PCS and yet are ready to do it again when the orders come—and they do come.
- They comfort and encourage one another when the going gets rough and there seems to be no smooth road ahead.
- They are brave when facing the emotional pain of living with the aftermath of PTSD.
- They tackle tough situations with kids who struggle when a parent is deployed multiple times.
- They do with less, and count it all a blessing, when money doesn't stretch until the next paycheck.
- They use humor to defuse hardships.
- They grieve for one another with compassion and understanding that is well beyond their years.
- They pray with conviction and confidence that would move mountains.
- They fight for their marriages, many of which are strained by continual separations.
- They understand what it means to sacrifice for their country.
- They live out the phrase, "We're in this together."

- They pull themselves up by their bootstraps, throw their shoulders back, lift their heads high, and press on each day as proud military spouses.

On the Move Again

Brenda, a Navy spouse, offers a glimpse into her life:

I was growing weary of the upheaval these moves brought into my life. This was our eighth move in nine years and was only a fifteen-month assignment. How many more times could I do this?

There has been a major difference in the manner in which I have been able to handle these most recent transitions. I am finally learning to cling to God's past faithfulness and to yield to His leading.

That's not to say that God has suddenly made moving a breeze. The circumstances continue to be as challenging as before. It's still difficult to leave behind a beloved home, familiar neighborhood, and dear friends. I still get a tight feeling in my chest each time my husband starts talking about a new set of orders. But I can honestly say that my attitude is changing, and in those moments when I remember to yield to God and His way, it has made a difference in how I have coped.

"For I know the plans I have for you, says the Lord. They are plans for good and not for evil, to give you a future and a hope" (Jeremiah 29:11, TLB).

God's plan for me to move all over the country (and even go to another part of the world) was not a plan to harm me, but a loving plan to draw me to a deeper dependence on Him. And His work is still in progress. I don't know how soon or how many more times I will be packing boxes and moving on. But I do know that I can count on God's faithful promise to lead the way through every challenge and circumstance and to provide for my every need in His perfect way.

Then there is Christy's poignant e-mail:

Do you know what it's like to follow your husband into strange territory like Sarah followed Abraham? Well, I do.

My husband is in the Air Force and has been for almost nineteen years. We move every two or three years. In those nineteen years, we have moved a total of eight times. We have lived in seven states and in Central America.

It is a lonely life sometimes. I have become very lonely for family and friends. When we are in a place where people are not sure how to treat military, I especially feel it. I sometimes just want to run home where I know people really love me.

Suppose Brenda or Christy and their families moved into your neighborhood, started going to your church or attending your schools? Would you reach out to them? Remember this chapter when you meet a military spouse and her family. I hope you'll go the extra mile to encourage them and express your appreciation.

The following suggestions come straight from what military women have shared with me. (Keep in mind, some of these can also apply to anyone who has moved.)

- While a greeting and smile are always appreciated, don't let it stop there. Be bold. Keep calling, encouraging, and inviting us to lunch, shopping, etc.
- Provide us with a list of local services: a handyman, mechanic, hairstylist, babysitters, churches, restaurants, etc.
- Offer to be our emergency contact for schools. That's the first question the schools ask and the one we never have an answer for.
- Offer to drive us to functions. We don't know our way around, and that would encourage us to go.
- Invite us to lunch or dinner after church on Sunday. That's a lonely day for us.

- Express your support. We appreciate hearing and reading your encouragement.
- Let us know you are praying for our service member and for our family.
- Please don't wait for us to ask or come to you. Knock on our door, talk to us at the mailbox, invite us over when we are out in the yard.
- My husband has his "niche" waiting for him. I have to build mine and help my children build theirs. Sometimes it's really hard. So I need "niche-building blocks" with friends and activities to help me build a new life in the community.
- We spend so much time making sure the kids are involved and busy, but we don't take care of ourselves during these transition times. I need to be included in Bible study, a girls' night out, a lunch group.
- Accept new military families as if they are moving in for a lifetime—not just passing through. I've seen it in your faces: *Oh, you're with the military. You'll move on. I don't want to invest my life or time in you.* Please invest time in us.
- Include us in neighborhood parties. Wear name tags. This helps us get to know people. Have a roster that people can fill out with names, addresses, phone numbers, and children's names and ages.
- People have picked up our check at a restaurant, or even paid for a cup of coffee, and said, "This one's on me. Thank you for your service to our country." It brings tears to my eyes every time. Our family is so grateful.
- Churches can be a great help in our transitions. They can schedule picnics, potlucks, or games at a park—anything that would welcome us along with other newcomers.
- Invite our kids over for a playdate.
- On special occasions or holidays at school or church, honor the dads or moms who are deployed. This means so much to our children.

- When my husband was deployed, a family in our church "adopted" our family. They cut the grass, helped out around the house, included us at holidays, and celebrated our birthdays. We will never forget them or what that meant to us.
- Pray for us. Ask about our specific prayer requests. Don't assume you know.
- Be understanding and be listeners. Sometimes our needs go beyond a plate of cookies.
- We belong to a culture that makes us somewhat isolated everywhere we go. We long to be accepted and included.
- Risk a broken heart. Love and support a military family even though we will eventually move and leave you. Allow your children to love ours as well, even though they may be sad when we leave.

So bring out your pom-poms and be their cheerleaders! Whatever works for you will surely work for them.

It's time to get off the bleachers and move from the sidelines to run with military families to the finish line.

If you're a military spouse, this chapter is meant to encourage you. My prayer is that it has, in some small way, let others see your life and your heart. I know you will have hundreds of cheerleaders across the miles, cheering you on.

Read on for some startling facts about our military families.[1]

1. A majority of military spouses are under thirty-five and female.
2. Only 5 percent of military spouses are men.
3. Nearly 20 percent of service members in Iraq and Afghanistan experience acute stress, depression, and/or anxiety.
4. Service members are more likely to be married at a younger age and have young children at home compared to their civilian counterparts.

5. Since 2001, more than two million American children have had a parent deployed at least once.
6. More than 900,000 children have experienced the deployment of one or both parents multiple times.
7. Children in military families experience high rates of mental distress and trauma. About 30 percent reported feeling sad or hopeless almost every day for two weeks during the past twelve months. Nearly one in four reported having considered suicide.
8. Approximately 37 percent of children with a deployed parent reported that they seriously worry about what could happen to their deployed caretaker.
9. Multiple and prolonged deployment also has an effect on spouses. Some 36.6 percent of women whose husbands have deployed report at least one mental health diagnosis compared to 30 percent of women whose husbands were not deployed.
10. Bereavement experts report that for each active-duty military loss, an average of ten people are significantly impacted. In the Iraq and Afghanistan wars, an estimated 68,360 family members were significantly affected.

CHAPTER 20

UPROOTED BY OTHER LIFE CHANGES

*I am not skilled to understand what God has willed, what
God has planned. I only know at His right hand is one who
is my Savior.*

DORA GREENWELL

HAVE YOU EVER BEEN blindsided by a major life change other than
moving? It can leave you numb, shocked, and devastated in a matter
of minutes. Your life, and everything in it, can change from being
complete to being crushed.

If you've experienced a life-changing loss, you know how hard it is
to pick up the pieces of a broken heart and a shattered world and try
to put life back together again. Those pieces will never fit together in
the same way. Life is forever altered.

After forty-five years of marriage I lost the love of my life, Bill, to
cancer. My only goal at that time was to breathe each day. Numb and
exhausted from grief and caregiving, I didn't know how to begin life
again. Each day as God breathed life in me, I learned how to cope and
adjust to my "new normal" as the healing process began.

When I wrote the three-step process for movers (let go, start over,
move forward), I never thought these principles would become part of
my healing process in the biggest life change I would ever face.

God knew then what I know now.

At some point, I had to choose to let go, start over, and begin to move forward with life after losing Bill. I reread my own book and, gradually, my heart began to rest in the biblical principles and Scripture passages I found there.

I soon realized that it was God's plan all along for those three steps to apply to other changes and losses that women face.

You might be experiencing the pain of loss by a different name. Perhaps it's the loss of your health, your marriage, a job, a relationship, a pregnancy, a dream to have children, a parent to Alzheimer's, a child to disease, a teen to drugs. It could even be a loss too painful to share. *You too, at some point, will have to choose to let go, start over, and begin to move forward with life.* Hard words to hear, but a reality we all have to face.

As you know, there are many uncertainties in a major life change. But this I'm sure of—you, my friend, are wrapped in God's comfort and strength each day. He covers you with His grace and mercy as you push on to survive.

Everything you have ever learned, experienced, and known about Jesus gives you strength for a time such as this. And if you don't know Jesus, you better not waste a minute getting to know Him now, because you need Him like crazy.

You can rest in His promises and rely on His Word for the days ahead.

You may be living with brokenness, but you can also live with a peace that is beyond understanding and a hope that is anchored in Christ.

There isn't a life change so traumatic that God cannot restore you, no pain so deep that God cannot bring you comfort, and no circumstance that is without God's presence.

Just ask the mom who lost her teenager in a fatal car accident and grieved as she clutched her Bible, open to Psalm 23.

Just ask the wife who divorced after thirty years of marriage and was able to give her husband the gift of forgiveness after years of his deception.

Just ask the young woman who had four miscarriages and yet never lost hope.

Just ask the family who lost their home in a fire and said, "God protected us; we praise Him!"

Just ask the military spouse who was able to pray for the enemy who took her husband's life.

There are countless more. Real stories, real lives. Women you and I have known. You've read their stories of triumph over tragedy. You may even know them by name. You may even be one of them. I've watched women like you rise from the ashes of despair to the beauty of hope. You were an encouragement to me in my darkest days.

When the Winds Blow

When your life has been uprooted by the winds of change, it can be only natural to feel like God has abandoned you.

You might feel as if He's the one who has left you—in the physical, emotional, or spiritual sense—when you need Him the most. Maybe you've wondered if He cares at all about you and your life.

Perhaps you think He's too busy with other things and other people. You could even feel that He's totally forgotten you, or worse, that He's simply ignoring you.

Funny how our minds can go off the deep end sometimes and we lose all sense of making sense, even when we really know better. Our emotions spill over into our thinking and reasoning. I know. I was a mess when Bill died.

Keep going back to Scripture. It will serve as a gentle reminder to ease your anxious heart and calm your thoughts in the midst of chaos and change. God's Word will reassure you that He has not, and will not, leave you.

Read the following verses out loud. Let the words penetrate your mind and heart. Hear God's voice speaking to YOU.

I am with you always, even to the end of the age.

MATTHEW 28:20

I will never desert you, nor will I ever forsake you.
HEBREWS 13:5

Then, when you call, the Lord will answer. "Yes, I am here,"
he will quickly reply.
ISAIAH 58:9, TLB

My presence shall go with you, and I will give you rest.
EXODUS 33:14

I will pray morning, noon, and night, pleading aloud with
God; and he will hear and answer.
PSALM 55:17, TLB

The LORD is near to the brokenhearted and saves those who
are crushed in spirit.
PSALM 34:18

When There Are No Answers

It's easy to lose perspective when you're in pain and hurting physically
or emotionally, isn't it? Life looks different through the grid of suffering. Oh, how quickly you can forget to rely on God's faithfulness
during those hard times.

Yet as I watched a friend go through immense physical pain as disease spread relentlessly throughout her body, I saw that the only thing
that got her through each day was her unwavering faith in God and
His promises. She had no assurance and no answers for the future, but
she chose daily to focus on Christ and not her pain.

The story of Job (see the book of Job in the Old Testament) can help
you stay focused and keep perspective at times in life when there are no
answers. Job lost everything: his possessions, his home, even his children. He also suffered from a horrible disease. Job asked "why" many
times. It is rarely easy to answer the "why" to our suffering, pain, or
hurt. We simply have to rely on God's promises instead of explanations.

Job came to understand God's faithfulness by trusting God. Job's faith was not in circumstances or in explanations, but in an all-powerful and all-knowing God. He wanted to reason with God, but He learned to rest in God.

My friend had the same faith and the same hope in God as Job did. She did not have the answers, but she had Jesus, and that was enough for her.

> After you have suffered for a little while, the God of all grace . . . will Himself perfect, confirm, strengthen and establish you.
> 1 PETER 5:10

> You who have shown me many troubles and distresses will revive me again, and will bring me up again from the depths of the earth.
> PSALM 71:20

God is with you—always, forever, and no matter what. He will not fail you or forget you in the days ahead. Choose to look up and not down, to look forward and not behind. In the midst of drought, He is your provider and source of living water that will never run dry.

One Day at a Time

I thought you might like to read a blog post I wrote soon after Bill died. It's the best way to reveal my heart and my thoughts at that time. May it be a testimony of our life and love together and a reflection of Christ through pain and suffering.

Dear Friends,
This is a new season of life for me as I face each day without Bill—my beloved husband, soul mate, and best friend. Forty-five years is a long time to be married; in fact, many of you aren't even that old yet, so it's hard to wrap your mind around what it's like to be married that long. We loved being together, and no matter where we had been,

the best part of our day was coming home to each other.
I was not only loved unconditionally, but felt honored,
valued, and cherished. It just doesn't get much better
than that.

Oh sure, we had some tough times together and there
were years that we struggled in our marriage. But as we
grew closer in our relationship with Christ over the years,
we grew closer in our relationship with each other and
worked through the difficult times. We were committed to
one another and our marriage, and God honored that over
the years.

As I watched Bill live four months with devastating
cancer pain and suffering, I also watched him live with
amazing hope, peace, and faith each day of his illness. How
Bill lived the last four months of his life was a testimony to
me, our children, and all those who came in contact with
him. When the hospital staff, doctors, and nurses would
ask him what he did, he would always say, "I'm a follower
of Christ." Plainly and simply stated, he reflected Christ
through his words, actions, and demeanor, even in his
darkest days.

Death came too soon and too quickly, and the impact
has shattered my world. Sometimes I trace Bill's face
with my hands in the air and feel his thick gray hair in
my fingers. The loss of his presence in my life seems
unbearable. The words "I miss you" are whispered daily
from the depth of my soul. The tears come unexpectedly
anytime and anywhere.

So, how am I doing? I'm doing one day at a time.
I choose to get up every morning. I choose to get
dressed, put on my makeup, comb my hair, and put on
a smile. I choose to teach my Moving On class at church
each week, go to the Just Moved Ministry office, attend
church on Sunday, and be with friends. I choose to be a
follower of Christ, even in my darkest days.

Standing on the Rock,

Susan

Let these reminders from God's Word speak to you when you need to stand on His firm foundation:

> He only is my rock and my salvation, my stronghold; I shall never be greatly shaken. . . . Trust in Him at all times, O people; pour out your heart before Him; God is a refuge for us.
>
> PSALM 62:2,8

> For You have been my stronghold and a refuge in the day of my distress.
>
> PSALM 59:16

His Mercies Are New Every Morning

A friend gave me a little wooden angel that sits on my kitchen counter. She has both arms stretched out and raised above her head as if to say, "Yes, I can!" Every morning when I walk into my kitchen, that little angel reminds me that I want to be a woman who, in the midst of life-changing loss, says, "Yes, I can!" I *can* be grateful for the immeasurable blessings in my life. I *can* focus, not on my loss, but on the faithfulness of God, and trust Him in *all* things. I *can* lift up my hands with thanksgiving and praise for a Savior who comforts and soothes me in my loss.

You can too.

God will not leave us or forget us. His mercies are indeed new every morning. Because of this, you and I can say, "Yes, we can!"

> *He giveth more grace when the burdens grow greater,*
> *He sendeth more strength when the labors increase;*
> *To added affliction He addeth His mercy,*
> *To multiplied trials His multiplied peace.*
> *When we have exhausted our store of endurance,*
> *When our strength has failed ere the day is half done,*
> *When we reach the end of our hoarded resources*
> *Our Father's full giving is only begun.*

His love has no limit, His grace has no measure,
His power no boundary known unto men;
For out of His infinite riches in Jesus
He giveth and giveth and giveth again.[1]

ANNIE JOHNSON FLINT

Here are some of the things I learned on my journey of grieving that you can apply to your life change. It starts with breathing.

Take deep breaths when you wake up in the morning, during the day, and when you wake up in the middle of the night. It helps to settle and steady your body and emotions. It also reminds you that you are alive.

Eat . . . yes, eat. You might not have an appetite or feel like eating, but you have to eat. Let your friends know that they can remind you to eat. My friends had to remind me daily.

Keep life as normal as possible with simple daily routines. If you work, you might need some time off, but get back to your normal routine as soon as possible. I resumed teaching my Moving On class at my church in September after Bill's death in August.

Take time for yourself. You're not being selfish; you're surviving. Do things that you enjoy. Pamper yourself. Take long walks and exercise. It's healthy for your body and emotions. I started working out at the YMCA. It has helped restore me physically and emotionally.

It's more than okay to ask for help. Life will be absolutely overwhelming if you don't. My church family and close friends became my go-to people, whether I needed a handyman or needed help with my computer or sprinkler system. All I had to do was ask.

Accept every invitation you get from people you feel comfortable with. Whether it's family, friends, or coworkers, just do it. The first time is the hardest, but you need their love, care, and support. I had to be talked into going to dinner with friends, but I was glad I went.

It's okay to cry, just don't get stuck there. Realize that the smallest thing can trigger your tears. Allow yourself to grieve and feel your pain. Know yourself well enough to recognize if you need grief support, counseling, or time with a close friend who will listen to your raw emotions.

Do the next thing, whatever that looks like. It's so easy to get overwhelmed with what seems like a hundred things that need to be done. STOP. Just do the next thing; that's enough for today. The next thing for me was as simple as watering my plants.

When friends ask you, "How are you doing?" answer, "I'm doing one day at a time." As interested and concerned as friends are, you hear the same question over and over again: "How are you doing?" My simple answer didn't require any more explanation and meant that I did not have to relive and repeat the details of my grief to everyone.

Your life may be reshaped by unexpected change, but it doesn't have to be defined by it. Bill's death certainly reshaped my life forever, but I am defined by Jesus Christ. I don't want to be known as a woman whose husband died. I want to be known as a woman whose faith, hope, and trust are in Christ.

Reach out to someone. You redeem your pain when you invest in the lives of others. Because you've been through suffering, you can offer the understanding and sensitivity that someone else needs. I invited a young woman, who had just lost her husband in a tragic accident, to join me for coffee. It was therapeutic for both of us.

And most of all, my friends, *saturate yourselves in God's Word.* Cover yourself with His promises. Wrap yourself in His love, comfort, and care. Run to Him in your loneliness. Soak up His presence. God is your lifeline of hope. Trust Him in all things. He is faithful. He alone will bring restoration and healing to your life.

This much I know.

FROM THE BEGINNING . . .

*What lies behind us and what lies before us are tiny matters
compared to what lies within us.*
WILLIAM MORROW

To UNDERSTAND THE heart of this book, you have to go back twenty
years with me. That's when it all began: the dream, the vision, and the
reality of starting a ministry for women who had been uprooted by a
move.

After moving fourteen times, I began grappling with the inconsis-
tency in my life. If you're a frequent mover, you get it. I was at the end
of myself when we moved to Phoenix.

God began to make obvious to me the three defining things I
needed to do in order to pull my life back together. I had to begin
to let go, start over, and move forward. These principles became the
theme for my life.

As I processed and worked through each one, God changed the
course of my life and prepared my heart for the inception of Just
Moved Ministry. If these steps helped stabilize me emotionally and
spiritually through the upheaval of a move, why couldn't they help
other women going through similar circumstances?

So began the dream.

At the time, many new people were coming to my church in Scottsdale, Arizona. Although we offered once-a-month coffee gatherings for newcomers, God nudged my heart with the question, *What's happening to these women after the coffee? Why don't we see them again?* I saw the need they had for weekly contact and support, the need for a place to belong, and the need for biblical teaching to help keep their focus on Christ. I knew it would be invaluable for these women to understand the feelings and emotions that accompany this change in their lives.

Why not offer a study group designed just for newcomers, give them a place to belong, and teach them biblical principles that would give them a solid foundation following a move?

So began the vision.

After much prayer and encouragement from friends, I started a little ministry outreach for newcomers at Scottsdale Bible Church. My journey through the three-step process became the basis for the class. With handwritten notes scribbled on notebook paper, I shared my story and walked the women through letting go, starting over, and moving forward with their lives after a move.

The Dream and the Vision Became a Reality

Our newcomers' group started to grow as more and more women came from all over the Phoenix area. People began to ask if I had given any thought to writing a book and teacher's manual so other churches could offer a newcomers' group.

The idea of writing a book and manual was beyond my wildest thoughts. My dream and vision for a ministry to newcomers in our church had become a reality. That was good enough for me. I was happy teaching and loving the women who came through each semester and watching God change their lives in the process. Little did I know what God had in *His* plans. The book talk continued and God planted more seeds of encouragement—and then more and more. The seeds started to take root and grow.

At last, my heart began to have a new dream and a new vision: to write a book and start a ministry for uprooted women beyond the walls of our church.

The Rest Is History

My scribbles on notebook paper became the catalyst for this book. It was published in 1995 by Focus on the Family, who understood the need for ministering to women and families who move. The Focus staff has become like a family to me. Over the years, they have extended kindness and thoughtfulness far beyond an author/publisher relationship. Some of the staff members have been my friends for twenty years.

After the Boxes Are Unpacked became the book that launched Just Moved Ministry, now reaching uprooted women and their families around the world.

With a desk, a phone, an antiquated desktop computer, a few manila file folders, and one volunteer, I opened an office at home in my guest bedroom. Books were stored in my garage. I would take an order, pack the materials, run to the post office and mail it. And yes, I did write a teacher's manual to accompany the book, as well as a workbook for the women taking the study.

Today, donor-supported Just Moved Ministry is housed in a seven-room suite in a small office building with eight part-time staff members and more than twenty-five volunteers.

God has done great things for us and we are filled with joy—every day! (Paraphrased from Psalm 126:2.)

Twenty Years and Counting

In 2015 Just Moved Ministry celebrated twenty years of bringing hope to uprooted women. God has enlarged my dream and vision beyond anything I could have imagined. He has used this book and our ministry to "move" thousands of women worldwide closer to Him. No matter where women come from, whatever their backgrounds, ages, or stages of life—the biblical principles apply. The message is timeless and has held true for all these years.

Churches across the nation and around the world soon recognized the impact Just Moved Ministry had on outreach, evangelism, and church growth by offering our studies. Soon after these studies spread into churches, they began to be offered in military chapels, mission and ministry organizations, seminaries, neighborhoods, faith-based companies, and among corporate expats.

Our outreach has expanded beyond our Moving On After Moving In groups. The JustMoved.org website encourages, equips, and embraces all women who move and is especially helpful to those living in remote areas of our world.

Resources produced by Just Moved Ministry have expanded to include more products geared specifically toward the uprooted woman and her family. New encouragement and practical tips appear regularly at JustMoved.org, which also offers ways for uprooted women to find each other within their new communities. A dedicated prayer team responds to hundreds of prayer requests.

Changed Lives

I've received so many endearing stories and heartwarming testimonies over the years. I've kept them all. Each is a story that unfolds chapter by chapter, year by year to reveal hope in God and His faithfulness to women at a time when they needed Him desperately. I see His healing love, His restoration, and the awareness of His presence in every story. Here are glimpses into a few changed lives.

"When my husband and I moved, I joined the Moving On study at our church. It gave me permission to grieve so many losses that this move brought to my life. I didn't even know I needed to grieve, but I did. *After the Boxes Are Unpacked* brought such healing and growth for me, and reading it gave me the desire to grow near to my Lord. Every woman in my group has also grown, and I am grateful to have had a glimpse into their lives and the privilege to see how our wonderful Jesus is intimately involved with each of us." —*Alicia from Tennessee*

"I just finished taking the class Moving On After Moving In, and I have to tell you that it saved my life! I happened upon the church that offered this class by mistake one day, but I am so thankful the Lord pointed it out to me. Through the book, I learned to rise above my circumstances. I began to focus my life on God, on my husband, and on my new baby. I found that once my perspective and goals were in line with God, my life began to fall into place. While I still struggle with being away from family and friends, I am so much more at peace. I learned how to deal with my emotions instead of keeping them inside and then exploding all over my loved ones. Thank you for your direct approach to this subject. Your words of encouragement in the book and your ministry reawakened my love for Christ. I am living proof that this ministry touches lives every day." —*Melissa from Nebraska*

"We moved from Indonesia to Peru, and have just moved to Ghana. I am so very thankful for finding out about your book and ministry when I lived in Peru. This move has been harder for me than the others. I know that I could not have made it this far without your book *After the Boxes Are Unpacked* and my Bible. I'm leaning on your materials and God's Word to help me get through this time. I feel so disconnected from everyone and from not having some expat friends close by. I know I can do this; I just have to be patient, keep the faith, and keep practicing all the things you said in the book." —*Lori from Ghana*

"I just wanted to say how very much I appreciate your ministry and the way that it has blessed my own family as well as my church family. My wife came from a military family, as well as a pastor's family, and moved often. We have had some difficult moves as a couple. This book blessed her and our entire family. As she applied what she learned and began to share it with others, it has further blessed our church and our community." —*A pastor from Florida*

"I just finished reading your book *After the Boxes Are Unpacked.* When I first heard of your book a year ago, I was rather arrogant and prideful and thought, *What a good idea to write a book for the novice mover. I am a military wife. I don't need to read that book, because I move often and I can handle it.* Well, we just finished our seventh move—and I needed your book. When I started on the first chapter, the tears came. It was like sitting down with a good friend and sharing the heartache of a move. It was encouraging to know that what I was feeling during this move was normal. I was allowed to grieve, not just for this most recent move, but for the ones in previous years as well." —*Kathy, a military spouse*

As I read over this chapter, I'm overwhelmed. I am in awe of all that God has accomplished—not because of me, but because of Him. I never imagined I would write a book, much less start a ministry that has an outreach for Christ all over the world. I never imagined *After the Boxes Are Unpacked* would still be in print after twenty years! But then I've learned never to underestimate our almighty God. I am an ordinary, imperfect woman whom God chose many years ago to do an extraordinary work in His kingdom, for His glory, according to His plan. I am merely His vessel, filled with His grace and mercy. I stand on the sidelines in amazement as I watch Him continue to work in my life, and now in yours. *To God be the glory! Great things He has done!*

Additional Tips
from Women Who Have Moved

"Hang in there. Cry as much as you want, but not all the time in front of your kids. Make your needs known, but realize that it may be God who meets them and not your husband. Get a map. Look out the window. Explain to your kids what's going to happen. Pray and be honest with God. He can take it. Don't think of it as being lost; think of it as exploring. If you don't like the first doctor you go to, try another one. This goes for restaurants, grocery stores, dry cleaners, and friends. Take a bath. Get a manicure. Cry. Laugh. Go to garage sales. Take yourself to lunch. Find things to be thankful for. Buy yourself flowers for the kitchen. Teach your kids how to cook." —*Dianna H.*

"Don't expect too much from yourself or your family. Everything is affected when you move. Realize you may be on an emotional roller coaster, so develop your sense of humor! Don't try to anticipate what may happen tomorrow or next week. Just live in today." —*Judy W.*

"Trust God . . . even when it seems that everything is mixed up." —*Julie M.*

"Enjoy each day. Focus on being rather than doing. Admit the loss you feel, give it to the Lord, and move on." —*Teri C.*

"Don't withdraw into the four walls of your house. You will have to make the effort to fit into the community and you will have to 'make the first move' toward making friends. People won't come knocking at your door. Use this time for growth. Leave your comfort zone. Discover the woman God wants you to be." —*Alma S.*

"Have a family prayer time. Share all your feelings. God will provide all that will be important for your family. Don't worry about anything (house, etc.). Put everything into your family and everything else will come together." —*Pam J.*

"Reach out to others. There are plenty of people more needy than you are. Get close to the Lord; He is all you will have in the beginning." —*Joan L.*

"Don't fight it. Submit to God—He knows what is best for you." —*Marian G.*

"Communicate daily with your spouse. Every few weeks ask each other, 'How are we doing?' Be honest with the Lord. It's okay to cry and have 'rainy days.' Create a home that is a haven for your family, a joyful place of familiarity. Get out and get involved." —*Debbie T.*

"Be prepared to be an initiator in order to build relationships. Find a church home. Exercise. Volunteer. Find a good hairdresser." —*Sudie A.*

"Accept it. Don't fight it. Trust in the Lord and know that this move is part of His plan for your life." —*Alma M.*

"Please learn that your security comes from Christ alone. The move is unsettling. Time will heal. Allow yourself to grieve your loss and to feel lonely. Look at it as an opportunity to have a new start and new friends." —*Robin A.*

"Don't expect too much too soon. Pray about everything. Listen to your children's needs and support your husband. Get involved. Pace yourself in getting your house finished. Remember, Rome wasn't built in a day!" —*Beverly H.*

"Try not to compare. Be patient. Reach out." —*Joan M.*

"Open your heart to a friend; she probably needs one too. Be patient; you won't click with everyone, but God will have someone special waiting." —*Debby A.*

"Work on completing projects. Ask a lot of questions. Exercise regularly. Believe and trust that God has good things in store for you. Dwell on the positive." —*Gina A.*

"Treat yourself to an ice-cream cone." —*Betty M.*

"Refer to your new residence as 'home' as soon as you move. I really think this helps a person let go of the past and move into the present." —*Karen O.*

"Stop and smell the flowers. Reach for the stars. Embrace life. Hold on to that which is most dear. Seize the day. Remember to say 'I love you.' Start a tradition. Enjoy the simple things. Don't complicate life. Bounce back. Redefine your life. Look at the big picture, not just the corner you're in. Laugh. Choose joy. Bake brownies. Put a bird feeder outside your window. Be flexible. Remember each day is a fresh start. Count your blessings. Put out a welcome mat. Say your prayers every night." From my heart to yours—*Susan M.*

The Nitty-Gritty of Getting Settled

I need to focus on how I can get it done,
and not bemoan the fact that I have to do it.
DIANNA, *a moving friend*

AFTER MOVING to Phoenix from Alabama, Connie said in desperation, "I need all the help I can get! I have so many things to do and so many questions to ask. I don't know where to begin. Can you help me?"

So many times when you move, there isn't anyone around to serve as a resource person for all that needs to be done and learned. If you're like me, and your mind is on overload anyway, all suggestions and ideas are greatly appreciated. That's what this chapter is about—practical suggestions to make your transition easier and to help you settle in.

First of all, remember that you've got a lot going for you as a newcomer in town.

Some of the Advantages of Being New
- You have the chance to start over.
- You will be known for the person you are now, not the person you were in the past.
- You have more control over your time because your calendar is not full . . . yet.
- You have an opportunity to change old labels you've worn.
- You can break old habits.
- You have the opportunity to reinvent yourself.
- Nobody has seen your wardrobe.

- Not only your clothes, but all the things that are old to you, will be new to everyone else.
- You get to experience a new culture.
- You'll have new opportunities for personal and spiritual growth.
- You don't have to meet other people's expectations yet, because they don't have any.
- You'll find new educational and social opportunities.
- Your ideas and perspective will be fresh and new to everyone.
- You'll have the opportunity to reprioritize your life.
- Moving will broaden your horizons.
- You'll be able to see God at work in your life in new ways.
- Before you get too involved and busy, you can find the time to begin, renew, or revitalize your relationship with Jesus Christ.

You can dwell on all the positive ideas in the list above rather than on the negative things you may hear.

Now, your moving friends and I would like to share some of the things that we did to help us get settled.

Twenty-Five Things to Do to Help You Get Settled

1. Be prepared to be an initiator!

2. Find a church home if you haven't already.

3. Get a new driver's license.

4. Get new license plates for your vehicles.

5. Shop for insurance policies (especially car).

6. Don't forget to look into renter's insurance if you are temporarily or permanently renting.

7. Program your GPS with the addresses of places you want to go, or carry a local map in the car and highlight routes and places of interest.

8. Check online for services available in your area.

9. Go online to the chamber of commerce for all kinds of great local information.

10. Subscribe to, or download an app for, the local paper. You'll learn what's happening, what there is to do, and lots of local information. For example, when to plant what, how to make local dishes, and what events are coming up.

11. Check on places of interest within a day's drive from your city. Great for weekend exploring and entertainment!

12. Take a picnic to the nearest county or state park.

13. Locate the hospital nearest you.

14. Contact your church for the names of reliable babysitters.

15. Register to vote.

16. Go to the concierge at a local hotel to find out what sights and activities he or she recommends in the area.

17. Find out when garbage pickup is and what recycling procedures your new town has.

18. Introduce yourself to your mail carrier.

19. Check out banks. Service charges vary. Start checks with the same number you ended with at your last bank for continuity and to assure merchants of your stability.

20. It will help you feel established when you receive "real" mail. Sign up for things like address labels and free offers to be delivered to your new address.

21. Ask your neighbors to refer you to good service people (plumbers, electricians, etc.).

22. In case of an emergency, know where the water valves and the electrical box are located in your house.

23. Ask questions. People love to give their opinions and input.

24. Order or make your own "business cards" for identification:

The Smith Family
Bob, Jean, Billy, Betty

ADDRESS / E-MAIL   PHONE

25. Make a set of emergency numbers to keep in your phone and at home:

- School
- Work numbers
- Sitters
- Veterinarian
- Pharmacy
- Electrician
- Plumber
- Doctors: medical/dental
- Security alarm company

Of course, there are many more "to-dos" that you've probably thought of or have already done. Hopefully, asking your new neighbors the following questions will help you cover some more bases.

Forty Things You Need to Know

1. What are some local customs?

2. What do people do here for leisure or entertainment?

3. What foods are popular here?

4. What department store is most like my favorite back home?

5. Where does the school bus stop?

6. Is my yard used as a shortcut to school?

7. Where are outlets or bargain places located?

8. Where are the bike trails? Jogging trails? Walking trails?

9. What cleaners have one-day service?

10. Do you know a good handyman who will, for example, install ceiling fans?

11. Can you turn right on a red light here?

12. Can you recommend a pest control service?

13. Which hairstylist gives the best haircuts?

14. What's the price of a good haircut here?

15. Where's the best restaurant for breakfast?

16. Where's the best place for a lunch with friends?

17. Is there a place that serves afternoon tea?

18. Think of your own favorite restaurant questions.

19. Tell me where to go for child care.

20. Can you recommend any sitters?

21. Is there a florist in town who offers weekly specials on flowers?

22. What are the grocery store chains here?

23. Which grocery store has the best meats?

24. Where can I find my favorite regional foods? (Grits!)

25. Tell me about the churches in the area.

26. Is there a "neighborhood watch" here?

27. Which major companies are based here?

28. What's the main source of income for the city (tourism, farming, etc.)?

29. Is there a Christian radio station here?

30. What kind of public transportation does the city have?

31. Are there areas of town that we should avoid?

32. Are there places or areas I should tell my teenager are not safe?

33. Where's the best place to work out? Do they offer spin or Zumba classes?

34. Are there any ordinances or neighborhood covenants I need to be aware of (no parking on the street, etc.)?

35. Where is a good place for a mani/pedi?

36. Do you know a trustworthy cleaning service? What's the going rate?

37. Who is a good decorator? Have you seen his or her work?

38. What are some free local events and activities?

39. What day trips should I take to explore the state?

40. What is one thing you think I need to know as a newcomer?

A little tip from me to you: Don't try to ask all these questions in one day! Just be ready to ask, when the opportunity arises, about those things that will shape your lifestyle for the next few years. I suggest that you make a list of questions you want to ask. Get input on what your husband and children need and want to know. Always share what you learn with your family. Remember, they also need help in making the transition to a new place.

Make the most of all the opportunities available to you, whether you are in a city or a small town. Greet people with a smile and a positive attitude. Remember that each person you meet is a potential friend.

Notes

INTRODUCTION
1. David Ihrke, "Reason for Moving: 2012 to 2013," P20-574 (Washington, DC: US Census Bureau, June 2014), https://www.census.gov/prod/2014pubs /p20-574.pdf.

PART ONE
1. Ruth Bell Graham, *Clouds Are the Dust of His Feet* (Wheaton, IL: Crossway, 1992).

CHAPTER TWO
1. Miriam Neff, *Women and Their Emotions* (Chicago: Moody Press, 1983), 114–116.
2. Audrey T. McCollum, *The Trauma of Moving: Psychological Issues for Women* (Newbury Park, CA: Sage Publications, 1990), 71.

CHAPTER THREE
1. Paul Tournier. *A Place for You* (New York: Harper & Row, 1968), 162–164.

CHAPTER FOUR
1. David Ihrke, "Reason for Moving: 2012 to 2013," P20-574 (Washington, DC: US Census Bureau, June 2014), https://www.census.gov/prod/2014pubs /p20-574.pdf.

CHAPTER FIVE
1. Elaine St. Johns, "A Member of the Family," *Guideposts*, July 1989, 21–22.

CHAPTER EIGHT
1. Sylvia Fair, *The Bedspread* (New York: Morrow Junior Books, 1982).

CHAPTER NINE
1. Gail MacDonald, *High Call, High Privilege* (Wheaton, IL: Tyndale House, 1986), 58–59.

CHAPTER TEN

1. David Ihrke, "Reason for Moving: 2012 to 2013," P20-574 (Washington, DC: US Census Bureau, June 2014), https://www.census.gov/prod/2014pubs/p20-574.pdf.
2. Vance Packard, *A Nation of Strangers* (New York: David McKay, 1972), 4–5.
3. Ben Ferguson, *God, I've Got a Problem* (Ventura, CA: Regal Books, 1974), 43–44.
4. Anne Graham Lotz, *My Heart's Cry* (Nashville: W. Publishing Group, 2002), 183.
5. C.S. Lewis, *The Problem of Pain* (1940, repr., San Francisco: HarperSanFrancisco, 2001), 91.
6. Elisabeth Elliot, *Loneliness* (Nashville, TN: Oliver-Nelson Books, 1988), 158.

CHAPTER ELEVEN

1. Margery Williams, *The Velveteen Rabbit* (New York: Simon and Schuster, 1983), 5–6.

CHAPTER TWELVE

1. Susan Miller, *But Mom, I Don't Want to Move!* A Focus on the Family book (Carol Stream, IL: Tyndale House Publishers, 2004), 78.

CHAPTER THIRTEEN

1. John Trent, *LifeMapping* (Colorado Springs, CO: Focus on the Family, 1994), 206.
2. Susan Mernit, quoting Marilyn Segal in "Good-bye House," *Parents Magazine*, May 1990, 117.
3. Shelly Miller, *Include Your Children in Life-Changing Decisions. Leadership Journal*, September 29, 2014, http://www.christianitytoday.com/gifted-for-leadership/2014/september/include-your-children-in-life-changing-decisions.html.
4. Lawrence Kutner, "Parent & Child," *The New York Times*, January 18, 1990.
5. Susan Mernit, quoting the American Association for Counseling and Development in "Good-bye House," *Parents Magazine*, May 1990.

CHAPTER FOURTEEN

1. Dee Brestin, *The Friendships of Women* (Wheaton, IL: Victor Books, 1988), 16.
2. Kathy Narramore and Alice Hill, *Kindred Spirits* (Grand Rapids, MI: Zondervan, 1985), 28.
3. Jerry White and Mary White, *Friends & Friendship* (Colorado Springs, CO: NavPress, 1982), 13.

CHAPTER FIFTEEN

1. Darien B. Cooper, *The Beauty of Beholding God* (Wheaton, IL: Victor Books, 1982), 11.
2. Tim Hansel, *You Gotta Keep Dancin'* (Elgin, IL: David C. Cook, 1985), 54–55.
3. Ibid., quoting Paul Sailhamer, 54.

CHAPTER SIXTEEN

1. Earl Wilson, *Self-Discipline* (Portland, OR: Multnomah Press, 1983), 6.
2. Jesus Jimenez, "10 Unforgettable Quotes by Jim Rohn," *Success*, September 16, 2014, http://www.success.com/article/10-unforgettable-quotes-by-jim-rohn.
3. Charles L. Wallis, quoting Henry David Thoreau in *The Treasure Chest* (New York: Harper & Row, 1965), 135.
4. Joseph Allison, *Setting Goals That Count* (Grand Rapids, MI: Zondervan, 1985), 20–21.
5. Oswald Chambers, *My Utmost for His Highest* (Westwood, NJ: Barbour and Company, 1963), 127.

CHAPTER SEVENTEEN

1. Warren Wiersbe, quoting Oswald Chambers in *With the Word* (Nashville, TN: Oliver-Nelson Books, 1991), 362.
2. Jean Fleming, *Between Walden and the Whirlwind* (Colorado Springs, CO: NavPress, 1985), 64, 67.

CHAPTER NINETEEN

1. These facts are quoted or adapted from "11 Facts About Military Families," DoSomething.org, https://www.dosomething.org/tipsandtools/11-facts-about-military-families.

CHAPTER TWENTY

1. Annie Johnson Flint, "He Giveth More Grace," public domain.

About Just Moved Ministry

WHETHER YOUR MOVE WAS a welcome opportunity or a dreaded event, you face tremendous change and the daunting task of starting over in a new place. Just Moved Ministry is committed to the spiritual growth and emotional well-being of women who are uprooted by a move. Through biblical teaching and personal support, we prepare, encourage, and equip a woman to let go of the past, rebuild hope, and embrace her new life when she moves.

Uprooted women contact Just Moved Ministry for personal encouragement and turn to JustMoved.org for helpful resources, inspiration, encouragement, prayer support, and an online community.

Churches, seminaries, faith-based corporations, and military installations around the world offer the Moving On After Moving In study from Just Moved Ministry in an effort to bring the hope and encouragement of God's Word to the uprooted woman. Based upon this book, the study guides women through the emotional stages of a move, helps them become aware of opportunities for spiritual growth, and provides a rewarding way for them to connect in their new community.

For those who choose to start a Moving On After Moving In study, Just Moved Ministry provides all of the necessary materials, leader newsletters, and one-on-one support needed to make the study a success.

Susan Miller, America's Moving Coach® and president of Just

Moved Ministry, is invited to speak nationally and internationally at churches, women's events, leadership conferences, military installations, and for corporations that relocate their employees.

Send us your moving story and survival tips. Sign up for our mailing list by sending us your mailing and e-mail addresses.

For Susan Miller's speaking availability, go to www.SusanMiller.org.

Contact information and information about our resources can be found at www.JustMoved.org.

Just Moved Ministry is headquartered in Scottsdale, Arizona. E-mail the ministry at info@JustMoved.org.

This updated version of *After the Boxes Are Unpacked* reflects and supports Focus on the Family's Twelve Traits of a Healthy Family within the context of moving.

Twelve Traits of a Healthy Family from Focus on the Family

1. Strong marriage: Research indicates that a genuinely thriving marriage is the result of practical progress in several key areas of marital life that models for children key aspects of a healthy family.

2. Commitment to family members: A strong sense of commitment is the foundation for a strong, fully functional family.

3. Shared spiritual foundation: The family fosters a shared spiritual relationship.

4. Communication: Communication is a vital and critical aspect of a healthy family.

5. Connectedness/togetherness: Connectedness is defined as the degree of closeness/warmth experienced in the relationship that children have with their parents.

6. Honor: Placing high value, worth, and importance on each role in the family.

7. Resiliency: Family resiliency is the family's ability to cultivate strengths to positively meet the challenges of life.

8. Consistent expectations (rules) and discipline: Healthy boundaries and consistency are critical for the family to know and experience success.

9. Shared responsibility: By working together, family members can build and maintain close relationships during periods of normal family functioning as well as during times of stress.

10. Healthy individuals: A healthy family allows each person to grow personally within the context of their role and within the context of Christ's calling on their life.

11. Community-minded worldview: Strong families are connected to the community and involved in community organizations.

12. Life/social skills: Families are intentional in passing down the critical aspects of skills needed for success in interpersonal relationships, work and Christian ethics, leadership, and calling.

For more information, visit focusonthefamily.com.